401(k) Plans

2ND EDITION

Editor's Update

(PPN: 5437-0102 — ISBN: 0-7931-2528-6)

In August 1997, the Taxpayer Relief Act of 1997 (the Tax Act) was signed into law amending several Internal Revenue Code provisions related to 401(k) plans. In October 1997, the Internal Revenue Service released its annual inflation adjustments for retirement plan limitations. To the extent these affect the content of this book, they are noted below.

Note: If you are taking this course through our Supervised Study program for continuing education or other credit, you will not be tested on this new information.

Limitation on exclusion for elective contributions raised

The maximum exclusion for employee contributions to a 401(k) plans is increased to \$10,000 (up from \$9,500 in 1997). Other limitations applicable to 401(k) plans were unchanged by inflation. For 1998, maximum annual additions to the plan remains at \$30,000, the limit on the amount of compensation that may be considered in computing contributions remains at \$160,000, and the contribution limit for SIMPLE plans remains at \$6,000.

Repeal of 15 percent excess distribution and retirement accumulation taxes

Under prior law, a 15 percent excise tax was imposed on distributions from qualified retirement plans, tax-sheltered annuities, and IRAs that exceeded \$160,000, or five times this amount for lump-sum distributions. An additional 15 percent estate tax was imposed on the excess accumulations remaining in these accounts at death. The Tax Act has repealed these taxes for excess distributions received after December 31, 1996 and for decedents dying after 1996.

401(k) plan investment diversification

The Tax Act prohibits companies from requiring employees to invest more than 10 percent of their section 401(k) elective deferrals and any earnings thereon in employer stock or assets. The change does not apply to employer-matching contributions, to ESOPs or to plans requiring no more than 1 percent of the employee's deferrable compensation to be invested in company stock. Also, employees are not prohibited from making a voluntary election. This provision applies to plan years beginning after 1998.

Tax on nondeductible contributions

Employers can deduct contributions to qualified plans, subject to certain limits. If contributions exceed these limits, a 10 percent nondeductible excise tax is imposed. However, contributions to defined contribution plans that are not deductible because they exceed the combined plan deduction limit are no longer subject to the 10 percent tax, to the extent that contributions do not exceed (1) the amount of the employer's matching contributions, plus (2) the elective deferral contributions to a section 401(k) plan.

The combined plan deduction limit applies to employers who maintain both a defined benefit and defined contribution plan to cover some of the same employees. In this case, for any given plan year, the total deduction for all plans is equal to the greater of (a) 25 percent of compensation or (b) the contribution necessary to meet the defined benefit plan's minimum-funding requirements for the year. The provision is effective for tax years beginning after 1997.

Rollover contributions

Plans receiving rollover contributions are in jeopardy of losing their qualified plan status if the rollovers received from another employer's plan do not comply with the qualified plan rules. According to IRS regulations, a recipient plan will not lose its qualified status if it can "reasonably conclude" that the distributing plan is qualified. The Tax Act directs the Secretary of the Treasury to clarify that it is no longer necessary for a distributing plan to have an IRS determination letter regarding its qualified status for the recipient plan to reasonably conclude that it is receiving a valid rollover contribution.

Paperwork reduction for employee benefit plans

Under prior law, plan administrators of employee benefit plans subject to ERISA were required to file summary plan descriptions and summaries of material modifications with the Department of Labor. These filing requirements have been eliminated so that effective August 5, 1997, employers must furnish these documents to the DOL only upon request. However, if plan administrators do not provide the documents within 30 days of request, a civil penalty of up to $100 per day can be imposed, up to a maximum penalty of $1,000 per request. If the failure to provide any requested material stems from matters reasonably beyond the plan administrator's control, no fine will be levied.

Prohibited transactions excise tax increased

Both the Code and ERISA prohibit transactions between tax-qualified retirement plans or medical savings accounts and certain "disqualified persons" such as plan fiduciaries and employers sponsoring the plan. Under existing law, a two-tier tax is imposed on such transactions. An initial tax equal to 10 percent of the amount involved in the transaction is imposed. If the transaction is not corrected within a certain period, a second tax equal to 100 percent of the amount involved can be levied. To further discourage prohibited transactions, the Tax Act has increased the initial tax from 10 to 15 percent, effective for transactions occurring after August 5, 1997.

Matching contributions of self-employed individuals

Under prior law, matching contributions made by an employer to a 401(k) plan on behalf of a self-employed individual were treated as elective deferrals. As a result, the total of a self-employed individual's elective deferrals and corresponding matching contributions could not exceed the limit on elective contributions ($10,000 in 1998). Effective for tax years beginning after 1997, these contributions will no longer be treated as elective deferrals.

SIMPLE 401(k) plan changes

Employer deductions: Previously, an employer could only take a deduction for contributions to a SIMPLE 401(k) plan equal to 15 percent of plan participants' total compensation for the year. However, for tax years after 1996, the Tax Act has effectively increased the amount that an employer can deduct. An employer can now take a deduction equal to the greater of (1) 15 percent of the compensation paid or accrued during the tax year to participants in a stock bonus or profit-sharing plan or (2) the amount that it must contribute to the SIMPLE 401(k) plan for the year.

Cost-of-living adjustments: An employee's elective deferrals to a SIMPLE 401(k) cannot exceed $6,000 each year. The Tax Act clarifies that this annual limit will be adjusted for cost of living increases in $500 increments. As noted above, however, no adjustment is being made for 1998.

Top-heavy exemption: A qualified plan will be considered top-heavy if the total of the key employees' account balances exceeds 60 percent of the total of all employees' account balances under the plan. If a plan is determined to be top-heavy, the sponsoring employer must make a minimum contribution of 3 percent of compensation for each participating employee who is not a key employee. The Tax Act clarifies that the exemption from the top-heavy rules only applies to SIMPLE 401(k) plans and not to other 401(k) plans.

Election requirement: Each eligible employee can make or modify an elective deferral during the 60-day period before every January 1. When an employee first becomes eligible to participate in a SIMPLE 401(k) plan, the employee must have the opportunity to make an election during a 60-day period that includes either the date the employee became eligible or the previous day.

Notification requirements: An employer maintaining a SIMPLE 401(k) plan must also notify each eligible employee of the right to make or modify an elective deferral during the 60-day period noted above. The notice must be provided a reasonable period of time before the 60-day period during which an employee can make or modify salary reduction elections. Employers must include a copy of the summary description prepared by the trustee with the notice. Also, the employer must specify whether it will provide a 3 percent matching contribution or 2 percent nonelective contribution.

Termination Requirements: An employee can terminate participation in a SIMPLE 401(k) plan at any time during the year. However, if the employee later wants to resume participation, the plan can prohibit the employee from doing so until the start of the next calendar year.

December 1997

401(k) PLANS

2ND EDITION

Dearborn
Financial Publishing, Inc.®

Published by Dearborn Financial Publishing, Inc.®

Printed in the United States of America.

Second printing, December 1997

Library of Congress Cataloging-in-Publication Data

401(k) plans. -- 2nd ed.
p. cm.
ISBN 0-7931-2528-6 (pbk.)
1. 401(k) plans -- Law and legislation. 2. 401(k) plans.
I. Dearborn Financial Publishing.
KF3517.Z9A15 1997
344.7301'2164--dc21 97-20066
CIP

Table of Contents

Introduction

Many people realize that the retirement income provided through Social Security and personal savings is simply not enough for them to maintain a comfortable standard of living after retirement. The inadequacy of personal savings and Social Security as sources of retirement funds places a greater share of the burden on employer-provided benefits. However, this is an increased burden that many employers are unable or unwilling to bear. Fringe benefits, including retirement plans, often cost an employer from 25 to 50 percent of an employee's salary.

What employers need is a cost-effective way to provide employees with a tax-advantaged method of saving for retirement. Such a plan does exist—the tax-qualified cash or deferred arrangement (CODA), popularly known as a *401(k) plan* after the Internal Revenue Code section authorizing it.

The number of 401(k) plans has exploded over the past decade. By any measure, the popularity of 401(k) plans is remarkable. Even in a time of change and cutbacks, the 401(k) plan is becoming a fixture in many benefits packages.

The purpose of this text is to provide you with an overview of the important concepts involving 401(k) plans. Among other things, this course will cover how a 401(k) plan works, how to tailor a plan for differing needs and requirements, what to look for in marketing a 401(k) plan and 401(k) plan administration and installation. The new SIMPLE plans created by recent legislation will also be discussed. These plans may be appropriate for small employers that do not have the resources to install and administer a formal 401(k) plan.

By the conclusion of this text, you will have a working understanding of:

- qualified retirement plans with 401(k) provisions;
- qualification requirements;

- contributions;
- withdrawals and distributions;
- plan loans;
- investment options; and
- reporting and disclosure requirements, such as filings with the Secretary of Labor.

From both the perspective of the employer and the employee, 401(k) plans provide a valuable benefit. For employers, 401(k) plans are a relatively easy and inexpensive way to offer retirement benefits to employees. For employees, 401(k) plans make it possible to save for retirement on a tax-deferred basis. The material in this text will give you the knowledge to explain to your clients the numerous advantages of a 401(k) plan for both the employer and employee.

Genevieve M. Ferraro
Managing Editor

1

Introduction to 401(k) Plans

Retirement planning is an art that requires an understanding of taxes and their effect on earnings. Because of their income tax advantages, 401(k) plans have been enthusiastically received by plan participants. Employees recognize the advantages of reduced current income taxes and increased annual savings. Employers are treated the same as employees for income tax purposes in a 401(k) plan. Their contributions are tax deductible. In addition, through a 401(k) employers are able to offer their employees a cost-effective employee benefit. The goal of this chapter is to give the reader an overview of 401(k) plans from their early days to the present.

OVERVIEW OF 401(k) PLANS

A 401(k) plan is an employer-sponsored retirement plan that allows employees to make pretax contributions to the plan. By *adopting* a 401(k) plan, an employer provides employees with a way to:

- reduce taxable income
- establish a savings/retirement fund
- enable retirement savings to grow on a tax-deferred basis
- tailor the fund to their own goals

The 401(k) plan has proved to be tremendously popular with both employers and employees. Indeed, one of the most notable trends in employee benefits has been the

ILL. 1.1 ■ Increase in Popularity of 401(k) Plans

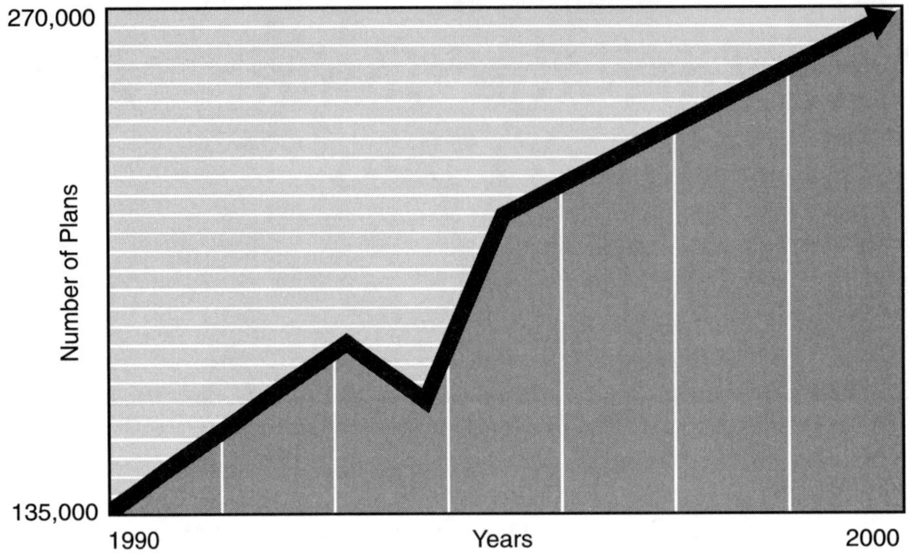

dramatic growth in the number of 401(k) plans. In fact, more than 90 percent of the Fortune 500 companies currently maintain a 401(k) plan. Few had such a plan prior to 1980.

But the most dramatic growth in the use of 401(k) plans is occurring among small to mid-size companies. Generally, small to mid-size companies are those with 25 to 1,000 full-time employees. More and more companies of this size will be setting up company 401(k) plans. In the next few years it is projected that the number of small company plans should exceed 250,000 with 3.5 million participants and $120 billion in assets.

HISTORY OF 401(k) PLANS

A 401(k) plan is a cash or deferred arrangement, whereby an employee can choose between taking his or her compensation in *cash* or *deferring* a portion of it until a later date, typically retirement. The money deferred is not considered taxable to the employee until it is withdrawn or distributed from the plan. Cash or deferred arrangements (CODAs) existed before the addition of §401(k) to the tax code. But the history of CODAs before §401(k) proved to be turbulent.

ILL. 1.2 ■ *Constructive Receipt*

Generally, a taxpayer who uses the cash basis method of accounting includes money in gross income in the year the funds are received and deducts expenses in the year they are paid. However, there is an exception to the general rule that income is not reported as part of gross income until the money is in the taxpayer's hands. Under the doctrine of *constructive receipt,* income not actually received nevertheless is considered to have been received constructively, or by legal interpretation, in certain situations. The law judges that income has been constructively received in the tax year in which it is (1) credited to the taxpayer's account; (2) set apart for the taxpayer; or (3) otherwise made available so that the taxpayer may draw upon it at any time. Income is not constructively received if the taxpayer's control over when the income can be received is subject to substantial limitations or restrictions.

The purpose of the constructive receipt rule is to prevent a taxpayer from receiving a tax advantage by deferring, entirely at his or her discretion, income to a later year when the tax liability will be less. For example, a taxpayer who would be in a lower tax bracket the next year might wish to postpone receipt of income until then.

The IRS several times reversed its position on whether money could be deferred to the CODA on a tax-favored basis. During the periods when the IRS's position was that tax-favored deferral was not available—that is, money an employee elected to defer would be currently taxable—the rationale was based on the doctrine of *constructive receipt.* The argument was that because the employee had the option to receive the funds in cash immediately, the amounts should be currently taxable, even if the employee opted to defer the income.

Congress generally opposed the IRS position that deferrals were constructively received, even blocking IRS efforts to issue final regulations supporting its position. Then, in the Revenue Act of 1978, Congress enacted §401(k) of the Internal Revenue Code ("the Code"). Effective for plan years beginning after December 31, 1979, the section provided that a plan should not be considered to fail qualification requirements merely because it permits a covered employee to elect to have the employer make payments as contributions to a trust or to the employee directly in cash.

Although the Revenue Act of 1978 formally permitted 401(k) plans and CODAs when it added §401(k) to the Code, it was not until after 1981, when the IRS issued guidelines for §401(k), that employers began to adopt 401(k) plans on a significant level.

Employers may incorporate a variety of elements into their 401(k) plans; however, certain features are common to most 401(k) plans. Most 401(k) plans include the following features:

- Employee participation is voluntary.
- The employee determines how much, within limits, to contribute to the plan.
- Employee elective contributions (or deferrals) and income earnings are not taxed until distributed.
- Individual accounts are maintained for each employee.
- Employees can choose how to invest their contributions among several different investment options.
- Employers match all or some part of employee contributions.
- Employer contributions, within limits, are tax deductible to the employer.
- Loans may be permitted.

■ ELIGIBLE PLANS

To establish a 401(k) plan, an employer must adopt a qualified retirement plan with 401(k) provisions. Alternatively, an employer may add 401(k) provisions to an existing, and eligible, qualified plan. Not every type of qualified retirement plan is eligible. A qualified plan is one that meets the qualification requirements in Section 401(a) and other sections of the Code.

A qualified cash or deferred arrangement, or 401(k) plan, must be part of a qualified *profit-sharing plan, stock bonus plan* or pre-ERISA *money purchase plan.* (The TRA '86 also provided that a 401(k) could be part of a rural electric cooperative plan.)

Profit-Sharing Plan

A *profit-sharing plan* is a plan established by an employer to enable employees or their beneficiaries to participate in the employer's business profits with a definite formula for allocating contributions and for distributing accumulated funds.

Contributions to a qualified profit-sharing plan no longer must be based on profits.[1] As a result, most employers are eligible for profit-sharing plans, thereby increasing the market for 401(k) plans.

Stock Bonus Plan

A *stock bonus plan* is one that provides employees or their beneficiaries with benefits similar to those in a profit-sharing plan, except that benefits are distributed in the form of employer stock. A stock bonus plan is basically an employee stock ownership plan (ESOP). An ESOP is a defined contribution plan that is a qualified stock bonus plan or a combination of stock bonus and money purchase plans designed to invest primarily in qualifying employer securities. Employer securities that may be used to fund an ESOP are employer common stock readily tradable on an established securities market; noncallable convertible preferred stock; and employer common stock not readily tradable if the voting powers and dividend rights are no less favorable than those of the employer common stock with the greatest voting powers and dividend rights. A special advantage enjoyed by ESOPs when compared to other qualified plans is that the employer may deduct, within limits, the fair market value of any stock contributed to the plan. No cash outlay is required to make a contribution, so capital may be retained for expansion or other business purposes.

Money Purchase Plan

A 401(k) plan also may be part of certain *money purchase plans*. A money purchase plan is a defined contribution plan under which a specific annual contribution is made by the employer and in which employee benefits are directly related to the size of contributions and the length of service. Only money purchase plans in existence on June 27, 1974, are eligible to contain 401(k) provisions. That was the date of the passage of the Employee Retirement Income Security Act (ERISA).

■ SUMMARY

A 401(k) plan is the name commonly used for a "cash or deferred arrangement" permitted under Section 401(k) of the Internal Revenue Code. Authorized under the Revenue Act of 1978 and amplified by later IRS Regulations, a 401(k) plan must be part of a qualified profit-sharing, stock bonus or pre-ERISA money purchase plan. Over the past decade the number of 401(k) plans has exploded. This popularity is due

1. Prior to TRA '86, contributions to a profit-sharing plan had to be made out of current or accumulated profits. This restriction meant that companies that were not profitable, such as those just getting started, were unable to establish this type of retirement plan.

primarily to the 401(k) plan options which provide considerably more flexibility for the plan sponsor and its employees than conventional pension plans. In the following chapter this course will examine the basic components of a 401(k) plan as well as advantages to the employer and employee.

CHAPTER 1 QUESTIONS FOR REVIEW

1. Which of the following terms applies to 401(k) plans that allow employees to make pretax contributions to the plan?

   A. Government-sponsored
   B. Employer-sponsored
   C. State-sponsored
   D. IRS-sponsored

2. 401(k) plans provide employees with a way to accomplish all of the following EXCEPT

   A. reduce taxable income
   B. establish a savings/retirement fund
   C. completely eliminate personal income taxes
   D. enable retirement savings to grow on a tax-deferred basis

3. A new form of 401(k) plan created for businesses with 100 or fewer employees and no existing retirement plan is known as a(n)

   A. individual retirement account
   B. QTIP plan
   C. SEP plan
   D. SIMPLE plan

4. For purposes of establishing a 401(k) plan, which of the following would NOT be considered an eligible, qualified plan?

   A. Profit-sharing plan
   B. Stock bonus plan
   C. Individual retirement account
   D. Pre-ERISA money purchase plan

5. Which of the following provides employees or their beneficiaries with benefits similar to those provided by a profit-sharing plan, except that the benefits are distributed in the form of employer stock?

   A. Stock bonus plan
   B. Pension plan
   C. Cafeteria plan
   D. Individual retirement account

2

Basics of a 401(k) Plan

Although the rules governing a 401(k) plan can become rather complex, the basic operation of the plan is nothing if not simple. The following three features are common to every 401(k) plan:

1. An employee may defer pretax income, up to $7,000 a year (adjusted annually for inflation), to the plan.

2. The employer also may contribute on behalf of the employee, up to a combined maximum of $30,000, without the employee's being taxed on the contributions.

3. The contributions are deposited into a trust account for the employee and grow tax free until distributed.

This chapter will review the basics of a 401(k) plan, concentrating on the advantages to employees and employers. Advantages to the agent or professional who works in the 401(k) plan market are also discussed.

401(k) PLAN ADVANTAGES

Search for the reason behind the rapid growth over the past few years in the popularity of 401(k) plans and you will discover that the answer is advantages. Employers do not establish 401(k)s and employees do not participate in those plans unless they are convinced that they will benefit. And both employees and employers realize significant advantages from 401(k)s.

Employee Advantages

The advantages of a 401(k) plan to the employee center around the favorable income tax treatment in storing dollars for future retirement. These advantages are shared with the employer, who, for purposes of the 401(k) plan, is treated as having the advantages of the employee.

Reduce Current Income Taxes. Because a 401(k) plan is a tax-qualified retirement arrangement, plan participants are able to reduce current income through 401(k) contributions and, as a result, reduce current income taxes. A 401(k) contribution is not deducted from income on the tax return, as in the case of an IRA contribution; rather the amount the employee elects to defer to the plan simply does not show up on the W-2 form as part of gross income. However, the contribution *is* included on the W-2 as a part of the wages subject to Social Security taxes.

Because the 401(k) contribution is not part of gross income, a plan participant can realize a significant decrease in income taxes owed. Let's consider an example that illustrates the difference a 401(k) contribution can make in current tax liability. Employees A and B both earn $60,000, are in the 28 percent tax bracket and each file joint returns. However, A participates in the employer's 401(k) plan; B is not a participant. In a tax year, A elects to defer $5,000 to his 401(k) account.

	Employee A	*Employee B*
Salary	$60,000	$60,000
401(k) contribution	$5,000	$0
W-2 gross income	$55,000	$60,000
Deductions/exemptions	$11,800	$11,800
Taxable income	$43,200	$48,200
Income tax	$6,883	$8,283

The 401(k) plan participant's tax liability is $1,400 less than that of the nonparticipant.[1]

Increase Annual Savings. Because 401(k) contributions are made with pretax dollars, the amount that an individual is able to save each year is greater with a 401(k) plan than with a savings account. For example, suppose that two individuals want to contribute $7,000 in pretax dollars for retirement. One of the two defers his income to a 401(k) account; the second deposits the money into a savings account. If each is in the 28 percent tax bracket, the individual with the savings account will be able to make an after-tax deposit of only $5,040, which is $1,960 (28 percent of $7,000) less than the amount the individual with the 401(k) account can contribute.

1. In the example, the tax is calculated using 1996 federal income tax rates. The deduction/exemptions calculation includes a standard deduction of $6,700 and two personal exemptions of $2,550 each.

	Individual A	*Individual B*
401(k) contribution	$7,000	$ 0
Savings account deposit	0	7,000
Non-deferred income tax at 28%	– 0	–1,960
Total after-tax retirement savings	$7,000	$5,040

Added to the difference in the savings because of the tax treatment of 401(k) plans are the employer's contributions to the plan on behalf of the participant. In many plans, the employer matches each dollar of employee contributions, up to a limit specified in the plan. These employer contributions result in the rapid growth of the account of an individual who is making full use of the savings opportunity.

Shelter Earnings from Taxes. Not only are contributions to 401(k) plans made with pretax dollars, but earnings also grow on a tax-deferred basis. No taxes are due on earnings, or pretax contributions, until they are distributed from the 401(k) plan, generally at retirement. Combined with the pretax funding of 401(k)s, the tax-deferred compounding of interest in the account ensures that a 401(k) will grow significantly larger over time than a traditional savings account, other factors being equal.

A graphic way to demonstrate the superiority of a 401(k) plan over a traditional savings account as a vehicle for retirement savings is to compare the results at various intervals. In the following comparison, two individuals, both in the 28 percent tax bracket, want to save $7,000 in pretax income for retirement. One individual deposits $7,000 in a savings account while the other places it in a 401(k) plan at his or her place of employment. The after-tax value of the savings account deposit is only $5,040 since the 28 percent tax on $7,000 resulted in a $1,960 reduction. The after-tax value of the 401(k) plan deposit remains at $7,000 because the income tax is deferred until retirement, when for most people their income tax rate is lower. If we assume each account earns 8 percent per year, the savings account interest, which is subject to current taxation every year, has an effective yield of 5.76 percent (8 percent – [8 percent × 28 percent] = 5.76 percent). The 401(k) plan is tax qualified and therefore earns 8 percent per year with no current taxation to reduce its effective yield. The difference after 20 years is significant.

	Tax-Deferred 401(k) Plan	*Taxable Savings Account*
After 5 years	$44,352	$29,904
10 years	$109,518	$69,471
15 years	$205,270	$121,824
20 years	$345,960	$191,094

Of course, the $345,960 represents the pretax value of the 401(k) account. Assuming a tax rate of 28 percent, the total tax owed would be $96,869. This leaves $249,091, compared to $191,094, in the savings account. This is a difference of almost $60,000.

ILL. 2.1 ■ *IRA versus 401(k)*

A comparison of maximum contributions to IRA plans and 401(k) plans and their growth at 8 percent annually.

	IRA Plan*	401(k) Plan**
After 5 years	$12,672	$ 44,352
10 years	$31,291	$109,518
15 years	$58,649	$205,270
20 years	$99,846	$345,960

*$2,000 contributed annually earning 8 percent. Contribution fully deductible.
**$7,000 contributed annually earning 8 percent.

Automatic Saving. In a typical 401(k) plan, the amounts that employees want to contribute are automatically deducted from their salaries. This arrangement provides the participant with a systematic and relatively painless way to set aside funds for retirement. Further, the plan frees the employee from any administrative paperwork in handling the savings account. All of that is handled by the employer.

Flexible Arrangement. Not every employee in an organization has the same needs and goals. Because the plan allows an employee to decide whether to participate and to what extent, subject to plan and legal limits and nondiscrimination factors, each individual is able to tailor the benefits to his or her specific situation. For example, a younger employee just starting out in a career may decide that immediate income currently is more important than future retirement benefits. As a consequence of that choice, the employee probably will elect to contribute less to the 401(k) plan than might an older employee who is closer to retirement.

Comparison with an IRA. An employee interested in setting aside income for retirement in a tax-qualified plan often must decide whether to start an IRA, join the 401(k) plan at work, or do both. Between these two types of qualified retirement plans, the 401(k) enjoys several advantages. First, the maximum deductible contribution to an IRA is the lesser of $2,000 or 100 percent of compensation. In a 401(k) plan, the employee can contribute up to $7,000, and that amount is adjusted annually for inflation. Even if an employee decides not to contribute more than $2,000 to a 401(k) that amount often will be matched by employer contributions. Matching is not possible in an IRA.

Other advantages of a 401(k) plan compared to an IRA include the following:

- The 401(k) participant may borrow from the plan without penalty if the plan permits. In contrast, a loan from an IRA plan triggers constructive distribution to the individual. The amount of the loan is included in gross income and taxed as ordinary income. In addition, there is a 10 percent penalty excise tax for premature distribution if the taxpayer is under the age of 59½. (However, the penalty tax will not apply if the distribution qualifies as an exception to the premature distribution rules.)

- The 401(k) participant may retire as early as age 55 and begin receiving retirement benefits without penalty. As noted above, there is a 10 percent penalty tax against distributions from an IRA before age 59½.

- Professional investment management is available without charge to the 401(k) participant. Although IRA funds can be put in a domestic trust or custodial account where the trustee or custodian may invest in a wide variety of assets, there is a charge for these services.

- The 401(k) participant may purchase life insurance in the plan, if offered. IRA money can be invested directly in individual annuity contracts issued by an insurance company, but they may not be invested in life insurance contracts.

Although the tax law does not prohibit an employee from having an IRA and also participating in the employer-sponsored 401(k), it may affect the employee's right to *deduct* IRA contributions. If a single individual who participates in a 401(k) or other employer-sponsored retirement plan has adjusted gross income (AGI) above $35,000, no part of the IRA contribution is deductible. If AGI is below $25,000, all of the IRA contribution is deductible. For individuals with AGI between $25,000 and $35,000, the amount of the IRA contribution that is deductible is reduced proportionately. For married, joint filers, if either spouse is a participant in an employer's plan, then the IRA contribution is fully deductible under $40,000 of combined AGI, not deductible above $50,000 and proportionately deductible between $40,000 and $50,000 of AGI.

An employee who both participates in a 401(k) and owns an IRA and who has income just above the contribution cut-off limit may become eligible for an IRA deduction because of the 401(k) contribution. For example, suppose that an unmarried taxpayer would have an AGI of $37,000 without the 401(k) contribution. If the individual makes a $5,000 401(k) contribution under a salary reduction plan, this would reduce AGI to $32,500, all other factors being equal, because the plan contribution is not included in current income. The reduced AGI would allow the employee to at least partially deduct an IRA contribution.

As you can see from Ill. 2.2, this taxpayer could deduct a $500 IRA contribution, thus reducing AGI to $32,000. In a 28 percent tax bracket, this additional reduction of AGI by $500 will result in an additional $140 tax savings.

Note that by reducing gross income and, consequently, adjusted gross income, the 401(k) contribution may increase those deductions that are eligible if they exceed a certain percentage of AGI. This type of deduction includes those for medical and

ILL. 2.2 ■ *Deductible Amount of IRA Contribution for Selected AGI*

Single Filer*		Married, Joint Filer**	
AGI	*Deduction*	*Combined AGI*	*Deduction*
$25,000	100 percent up to $2,000	$40,000 and under	$2,000
$27,500	$1,500	$42,500	$1,500
$30,000	$1,000	$45,000	$1,000
$32,500	$500	$47,500	$500
$35,000 and over	$0	$50,000 and over	$0

*IRA owner is a participant in a qualified employer-sponsored plan.
**IRA owner or spouse is a participant in a qualified employer-sponsored plan.

miscellaneous expenses. For example, only medical expenses that exceed 7.5 percent of adjusted gross income are deductible. If a taxpayer has medical expenses of $4,500 and an adjusted gross income of $40,000 without any 401(k) contribution, then only $1,500 of the expenses are deductible (7.5 percent × $40,000 = $3,000; $4,500 – $3,000 = $1,500 deductible medical expenses). If the taxpayer makes a $7,000 contribution to a 401(k), then $2,025 of the expenses will be deductible ($40,000 – $7,000 = $33,000; 7.5 percent × $33,000 = $2,475; $4,500 – $2,475 = $2,025 deductible medical expenses).

Employer Advantages

The advantages gained by an employer under a 401(k) plan fall into two categories: those that apply to the employer personally as an employee and those that apply to the business.

Employer as Employee. Because a business owner is considered an employee for purposes of 401(k) plans, the owner would enjoy all of the advantages discussed above, including pretax funding of the plan and tax-deferred earnings on the account.

Deductible Contributions. The tax advantages of 401(k) plans as they apply to employees have been discussed above. However, these plans also provide a tax incentive for employers: employer contributions are currently deductible. Deductible amounts include not only the employer matching contributions but also the money contributed by the employer on behalf of an employee under that employee's election.

Compensation paid by the employer to an employee as well as the amounts the employee elects to defer to a 401(k) plan are deductible by the employer. Thus, the

ILL. 2.3 ■ *If Tax Rates Rise*

As substantial as are the tax advantages of 401(k) participation, an employee might decide that it is smarter to pay taxes currently rather than deferring them to some future date. If the employer does not match employee contributions and if the employee does not believe that his or her tax rate at retirement will be much lower than the current rate, then it might be better to pay the taxes currently. (The lack of matching contributions is important in this decision, for matching contributions represent an immediate return on the amount the employee contributes in the plan.)

The concern of an employee about the retirement tax rate is based on predictions that the tax rates will be increased within a few years. However, to calculate accurately whether an employee will be ahead by paying the taxes currently, both the length of time the money will be left in the 401(k) and the tax rate at the time the money is withdrawn must be known. Because these are unknown factors, only rough estimates can be made.

If tax rates rise by the time the money is withdrawn from the 401(k) plan, and if that places the participant in a higher tax bracket, then it may be better for the participant to pay the tax currently at the lower rate than to wait for distribution at retirement when the tax rate is even higher.

For example, suppose an employee in the 28 percent tax bracket contributes $7,000 to a 401(k) plan and earns a pretax rate of 8 percent. Assuming no additional contributions, that $7,000 will grow to $10,285 after five years and to $15,112 after ten years. On the other hand, a taxable investment of the same amount at the same interest rate is initially reduced to $5,040 after taxes. Its after-tax growth will be $6,669 after five years and $8,824 after ten years.

The difference between the 401(k) investment and the taxable investment after five years is $3,616. If the previously untaxed 401(k) amount is withdrawn after five years, then the 401(k) will be a better investment only if the tax due on $10,285 is less than $3,616. Because $3,616 is almost 35 percent of $10,285, if the tax rate at the time of withdrawal is less than 35 percent, then the 401(k) is the better deal.

The same concept applies if the money remains in each investment for ten years. The difference between the 401(k) investment and the taxable investment after ten years is $6,288. If the 401(k) amount is withdrawn after ten years, it will be the better investment only if the tax due on $15,112 is less than $6,288. Because $6,288 is about 42 percent of $15,112, as long as the tax rate at the time of withdrawal is less than 42 percent, then the 401(k) is the better choice.

employer does not lose a deduction for the deferred amounts by establishing a 401(k) plan. In addition, any other funds contributed to the 401(k) plans are deductible, within the permitted limits. For example, if the plan calls for employer matching contributions, these amounts are also deductible.

Deducting employer contributions means that the federal government indirectly subsidizes the 401(k) plan. For example, if an employer is in the 25 percent tax bracket, a $1 contribution costs the employer only $0.75. The remaining $0.25 represents the federal government's "contribution" to the plan.

Cost-Effective Employee Benefit. Because all or part of an employee's benefits are funded by employee elective deferrals, a 401(k) plan offers an employer a low-cost way to provide a tax-qualified retirement plan. However, the administration expenses associated with a 401(k) plan often are larger than those of other plans.

Consider the situation where the employees contribute an average of 5 percent of salary to a 401(k) plan with the employer adding another 2.5 percent under a matching provision. Although the employer contributes only 2.5 percent of payroll above what it would have spent anyway (if the employees had elected to receive the money as current income rather than deferring it), a total of 7.5 percent of payroll is added to the employees' retirement accounts. If the employer had a non-401(k) defined contribution plan, it would have to contribute the full 7.5 percent of payroll in order to reach the same end.

Of course, the cost effectiveness of a 401(k), as demonstrated in this example, is offset somewhat by the larger administrative costs incurred by 401(k)s. These added costs are the result of the increased paperwork associated with tracking elective deferrals, matching contributions and investment performance in the various investment options. Still, the fact that the employees' elective deferrals finance all or a large part of the 401(k) contributions more than compensates for these increased employer costs.

Way to Recruit or Retain Personnel. The success of any business depends upon the caliber of its employees. An employer faces a constant struggle to retain valuable workers and to recruit others, a struggle also being waged by the employer's competitors. In that competition for quality personnel, an employer with a 401(k) plan in place enjoys a significant advantage.

Source of Increased Productivity. The existence of a 401(k) plan also may result in increased productivity on the part of an employer's work force. When employees understand the benefits of the plan, they are likely to respond by carrying out their duties more effectively. The personal financial security provided by the 401(k) reduces anxiety, enables the employee to concentrate on his or her duties, and results in overall increased productivity for the firm. Companies run efficiently and show profits when they command the mental concentration and physical drive of their key personnel.

Flexibility in Design. As discussed earlier, 401(k) plans are available in a variety of styles. This allows for the design of a plan that meets the employer's particular needs and objectives. The options available allow the employer the choice of having the plan financed by employee salary deferrals, with or without matching employer contributions; by employer bonuses; or by some combination of the above. The employer also has the choice of allowing or prohibiting hardship withdrawals and plan loans (both discussed later). The added paperwork involved in including one or both has to be balanced against the employee's desire to have access to the funds before retirement. As part of the design, the employer also must choose the investment options that will be offered to plan participants. The options included generally are broad enough to allow the employee to select one or more that best meet his or her own goals.

Advisor/Planner Advantages

The advantages of 401(k) plans are not limited to those enjoyed by employers and employees. An advisor or financial planner who works in the 401(k) plan market also benefits in a number of ways. Let us consider these benefits in terms of the market, potential rewards and the competition.

Market. The market for 401(k) plans will be covered in more detail later in this manual. However, for now, keep in mind that the potential market for these plans is enormous. When reading surveys about the popularity of 401(k) plans, a person might decide that most companies already have such plans. Not so. Those surveys generally concentrate on the large companies, but there are many more small and mid-sized companies, most of which do not have such a plan. Moreover, the creation of the SIMPLE plan makes businesses that employ 100 or fewer employees eligible to establish plans that operate like 401(k)s. Remember that the majority of employees work for these smaller firms.

Of course, the large size of a potential market does not mean that the market will be receptive to the product or service being offered by the seller. All too often the potential buyers simply are not interested in the merchandise. Happily this is not the case with 401(k) plans. The rapid growth in the popularity of 401(k) plans since their introduction demonstrates that the market is indeed responsive to the advantages offered by these plans.

Rewards. The potential financial rewards available in marketing 401(k) plans are not based only on the number of potential business clients but also on the number of sales that may follow the successful close of a 401(k) plan. Once the employer has decided to adopt a 401(k) plan and to include life insurance products as an investment option, the financial services professional has the opportunity to sell life insurance to each individual participant. In a small corporation, a financial services professional may sell a dozen or more policies as a result of successfully convincing the employer of the benefits of 401(k)s.

Competition. Obviously, the financial services professional who enters the 401(k) market will face competition, both from within and from outside the life insurance industry, but the competition may not be as extensive as one might think.

Other financial services professionals will be the main source of competition. However, it is important to realize that not every life insurance company is in the 401(k) market. This fact eliminates as competitors those financial services professionals representing insurers who are not in the market. Further, even if an insurer is in the 401(k) market, many of its representatives choose not to get involved in selling 401(k)s. Perhaps the major reason financial services professionals do not become involved with 401(k)s is the fear that the plans are too complicated. As the material in this manual will show, 401(k) plans are not simple, but neither are they incomprehensible. The financial services professional willing to put in the effort required to learn about 401(k)s will find the work amply rewarding.

Competition outside the life insurance industry is provided by bank trust companies. However, the life insurance industry enjoys a significant advantage in this competition because, unlike the trust industry, it has a field force to locate and sell prospects. Further, life insurance products provide a 401(k) plan with benefits not obtainable with other types of investments. As will be discussed later, these benefits include increasing participation in the 401(k) plan and providing a way for a participant to complete a savings program even if his or her career is cut short by an early death.

SUMMARY

As a qualified plan, a 401(k) plan produces significant tax advantages, including tax-deferred employee contributions and tax-deductible employer contributions. To remain qualified, a 401(k) plan must comply with a myriad of technical requirements. These requirements can be onerous and will be covered in the following chapters.

CHAPTER 2 QUESTIONS FOR REVIEW

1. Under a 401(k) plan, an employee may defer pretax income of up to which of the following amounts, adjusted annually for inflation, each year?

   A. $30,000
   B. $20,000
   C. $7,000
   D. $2,500

2. Which of the following is NOT an advantage for employees who participate in a 401(k) plan?

   A. A decrease in current income taxes
   B. A systematic method for setting aside funds for retirement
   C. A flexible retirement plan arrangement that allows employees to decide whether to participate and to what extent
   D. Tax-free distributions upon retirement

3. Which of the following statements concerning 401(k) plans and IRAs is true?

   A. Loans may be made from both a 401(k) plan and an IRA plan without penalty.
   B. Matching employer contributions are available with both 401(k) plans and IRAs.
   C. The deductibility of IRA contributions may be limited when an individual participates in both a 401(k) plan and an IRA.
   D. Both 401(k) plan participants and IRA owners may retire as early as age 55 and begin receiving retirement benefits without penalty.

4. A 401(k) plan provides the employer with each of the following advantages EXCEPT

   A. a cost-effective employee benefit
   B. a way to recruit and retain personnel
   C. the same advantages enjoyed by the rank-and-file employees
   D. a method of providing benefits only for the highly compensated

5. If an employee is in the 28 percent tax bracket and defers $5,000 of income to a 401(k) plan, that employee's current taxable income is reduced by how much?

   A. $5,000
   B. $1,400
   C. $3,600
   D. $0

3

Plan Design, Qualification Requirements and Contributions

The success of any good retirement savings plan depends on its flexibility to adapt to different situations. There are three broad categories of plans that meet the 401(k) definition, in addition to new hybrids being developed every day. However, qualification requirements must be met for any 401(k) plan type and there are limits on contributions to the plan. These are the subjects covered in the following pages: plan design, qualification requirements and contribution limits.

PLAN DESIGN

An employer who wishes to establish a 401(k) plan has a number of plan types from which to choose. The three main types are described below. However, these can be combined in a variety of ways to meet the employer's specific needs.

Savings Plan

The first option for the employer is to establish a *savings plan.* In this type of 401(k) arrangement, the employee makes all of the contributions to his or her individual account through salary reduction. The employee decides how much to contribute to the plan, within set limits, and this amount is transferred to the account by the employer on the employee's behalf. The deferred amount is not included in the participant's taxable income for income tax purposes, but it is subject to Social Security (FICA) and federal unemployment (FUTA) taxes as part of an employee's "wages."

Because all contributions to this type of plan are from the salary reduction of the participants, the savings plan option does not cost the employer anything, aside from administration expenses. This type of plan, therefore, may appeal to an employer who already has a qualified plan in existence and does not want to make additional contributions but who is feeling pressure from employees wanting to save additional amounts for retirement.

Cash Option Plan

In contrast to the employee-pay-all savings plan, the *cash option plan* involves only employer funds. The employer makes an annual contribution available to the employee who elects to take all, part or none of the contribution in cash and to have any remainder credited to his or her 401(k) account. The portion taken in cash is added to the individual's gross income for the year; the part deferred to the account does not show up as taxable wages on the employee's W-2 for that year. The deferred amount and its earnings are tax deferred until distribution. Notice that this type of plan does not involve any reduction in the salary of the participant. In fact, the employee's income increases by the amount of the contribution taken in cash.

The cash option plan allows the employee to decide how the employer's contribution is to be used, so this plan permits a great deal of flexibility. Employees who prefer more current income have the option to elect cash; those who want more funds set aside for retirement have that choice.

Thrift Plan

The third major type of 401(k) arrangement is the *thrift plan*. With this setup, which is a variation of the savings plan, the employer matches all or part of the employee's deferrals under a salary reduction election. For example, the plan might provide that the employer would contribute $0.50 for each dollar the employee puts into the plan. This type of matching arrangement is often included in a 401(k) plan as a way to increase employee participation.

■ QUALIFICATION REQUIREMENTS

For a cash or deferred arrangement to satisfy Code §401(k) qualification requirements, it must first satisfy the requirements in Code §401(a) applicable to qualified plans in general. This is in addition to meeting the special requirements for 401(k)s.

ILL. 3.1 ■ *The Typical 401(k) Plan*

		Percentage of Plans with this Feature
Level of Participation	The average participation rate is 78 percent.	
Eligibility	Participants are typically enrolled after a 12-month waiting period.	48%
Employee Contributions	The most common maximum pretax contribution permitted is 15 percent of salary (for plans with one maximum).	44%
	The most common maximum post-tax contribution permitted is 10 percent of salary (for plans with one maximum).	33%
	The most common maximum total contribution permitted is 15 percent of salary (for plans with one maximum).	41%
Employer Matching Contributions	The most common matching contribution is a fixed amount per dollar up to a maximum percentage of salary.	63%
	The most common employer match amount per dollar is $0.50 (for plans using the formula above).	54%
	The most common maximum percentage matched is 6 percent (for plans using the formula above).	43%
	Employer matching contributions are typically made with cash.	79%
Investments	Plan sponsors typically offer six options.	21%
	Employees are typically permitted to change investment elections for future contributions every pay period.	49%
	Employees are typically permitted to change investment elections for existing account balances daily.	53%
Loans and Withdrawals	The typical 401(k) plan has a loan provision.	86%
	Plan sponsors typically charge a fee for taking a loan.	62%
	The typical minimum dollar amount for taking a loan is $1,000.	72%
	Prime rate + 1 percent is the key indicator typically used to set the loan interest rate.	44%
	Hardship withdrawals are the most common type of in-service withdrawals permitted.	92%
Recordkeeping and Administration	Plan participants typically obtain account balance information via a voice response system.	76%
	Plan valuations are typically processed on a daily basis.	59%
	Plans are typically in compliance with ERISA 404(c) regulations.	83%

Source: BUCK CONSULTANTS

General Requirements

Included among the general requirements for qualification are the following:

- The plan must be written.
- The plan must be in effect.
- The plan must be communicated to employees.
- The plan must be established by the employer.
- The plan must be permanent.
- The plan must be for the exclusive benefit of employees.
- Contributions must be made by the employer, employee or both.

Participation Requirements

To be qualified, a 401(k) plan must allow any employee to participate who has completed one year of service and is at least 21 years old. One year of service means a 12-month period, measured from when the employee first becomes employed and during which he or she works at least 1,000 hours. Special rules apply where there is an absence from work due to pregnancy, childbirth or adoption. If an employee with one service year has not reached age 21, then the plan may exclude that individual until he or she reaches age 21. If the plan calls for 100 percent immediate vesting of employer contributions, the plan may require two years of service for participation instead of one. Vesting occurs when the employee's rights in employer contributions become nonforfeitable.

Employees meeting the plan requirements must be admitted to the plan no later than the earlier of: (1) the first day of the plan year following the date the employee qualifies; or (2) the date six months after the date of employee qualification.

The tax code also mandates that an employee not be excluded from plan participation simply because he or she has attained a certain age. A maximum age requirement for participation is not permissible.

Eligible Employee Defined

By definition, an employee eligible to participate in a 401(k) plan is one who can directly or indirectly make an election under the plan to take cash or defer it to the plan, for all or part of the plan year. An employee is not considered "ineligible" simply because he or she elects not to participate or cannot make a deferral election because of taking a hardship withdrawal.

Nondiscrimination and Coverage Requirements

Among the qualification requirements applying to all qualified plans is one that prohibits discrimination in coverage or in contributions and benefits. More specifically, a plan may not discriminate in favor of shareholders, officers or highly compensated employees—the *prohibited group.*

Highly Compensated Employees

The Code defines a highly compensated employee as one who:

- was a 5 percent owner at any time during the current year or the preceding year; or
- had compensation from the employer in excess of $80,000 during the preceding year and, if the employer elects, was in the top 20 percent of employees' compensation. (The $80,000 amount is adjusted annually for inflation.)[1]

Minimum Coverage Requirement

Once the number of highly compensated employees has been identified, the plan must satisfy a minimum coverage requirement. This requirement ensures that a certain number of nonhighly compensated employees, compared to highly compensated employees, are eligible to benefit under the plan. The coverage requirement is satisfied if the plan passes either the *ratio percentage test* or the *average benefit percentage test.*

Ratio Percentage Test. This test determines the ratio of nonhighly compensated employees who participate in the plan to highly compensated employees who participate. The ratio percentage for a plan year must be at least 70 percent. The ratio percentage is calculated using the following formula:

$$\frac{\text{Percentage of Nonhighly Compensated Employees Who Benefit Under the Plan}}{\text{Percentage of Highly Compensated Employees Who Benefit Under the Plan}} = \text{Ratio Percentage}$$

1. The $80,000 amount is adjusted annually for inflation at the same time and in the same way as adjustments to the defined benefit limit, which is $125,000. However, the base period will be the calendar quarter ending September 30, 1996.

Average Benefit Test. An employee's benefit percentage is his or her employer-provided contributions, under all qualified plans, calculated as a percentage of his or her compensation. Employee contributions are not taken into account in calculating employee benefit percentages. The average benefit percentage is the average of the benefit percentages calculated separately for each employee. The average benefit test is satisfied if (a) a plan passes a nondiscriminatory classification test (discussed below) and (b) provides an average benefit percentage for participating nonhighly compensated employee that is at least 70 percent of the average benefit for participating highly compensated employees.

The nondiscriminatory classification requirement of the average benefit test has two parts. First, the classification of employees must be reasonable, and reflect a bona fide business purpose for the classification. Second, the classification cannot be discriminatory. A safe harbor is provided under Code regulations for determining whether a classification is nondiscriminatory. Under the regulations, if a plan's ratio percentage (as determined above under the ratio percentage test) is below a specified unsafe harbor amount, the plan is discriminatory. If it falls between an unsafe harbor and safe harbor amount, the plan must satisfy a facts and circumstances test. According to the IRS, the exclusion of part-time employees from plan participation may be considered discriminatory and violate participation rules.

To illustrate the average benefit percentage tests, suppose that the average benefit percentage for the highly compensated is 6 percent, while the ABP for the nonhighly compensated is 4 percent. This plan would fail the percentage requirement of the test since the ABP for the lower paids is less than 70 percent of that for the highly compensated. The 70 percent test requires that the nonhighly compensated have an ABP of at least 4.2 percent (70 percent × 6 percent). In fact, the ABP for these employees is only 4 percent.

Vesting Requirements

With regard to qualified plans, including 401(k) plans, the term "vesting" or "vested" refers to how and when a participant acquires a nonforfeitable right to the benefits under the plan or the amounts contributed to his or her account. The 401(k) rules require that employee elective deferrals, or contributions, must be 100 percent vested at all times. That is, the employee's rights in the amounts deferred to the CODA under a salary reduction agreement and the amounts deferred out of a bonus may not be forfeited. With regard to employer matching contributions and any other employer contributions to an employee's 401(k) account, the vesting schedule specified in the plan must provide for vesting on terms that are at least as generous as the vesting schedules set out in the tax code. Remember that 100 percent vesting must be provided if the plan uses the two-year service requirement.

Five-Year Vesting. Under the five-year vesting schedule, no vesting is required before the participant has completed five years of service. After five years, 100 percent vesting is required.

Years of Service	*Percent Vested*
Under 5	0
5 and more	100

Three- to Seven-Year Vesting. This vesting schedule mandates that a participant be vested 20 percent after three years of service, with an additional 20 percent vesting for each additional year of service. A participant becomes fully vested after seven years of service. The following schedule illustrates 3- to 7-year vesting:

Years of Service	*Percent Vested*
Under 3	0
3	20
4	40
5	60
6	80
7	100

Alternatively, a plan could use another vesting approach as long as it is no less favorable to the participants than these.

TOP-HEAVY PLANS

A top-heavy plan is one in which the sum of the account balances of key employees exceeds 60 percent of the sum of all account balances under the plan. A key employee is defined as:

1. an officer of the company whose annual compensation exceeds 50 percent of the defined benefit annual limit in effect for that year (in 1996, this amount was $120,000; in 1997, it was $125,000);

2. one of the ten employees having annual compensation from the employer in excess of the defined contribution limitation (currently $30,000) and owning more than .5 percent interest and one of the ten largest interests in the company;

3. a 5 percent or greater owner of the company; or

4. a 1 percent or greater owner receiving annual compensation in excess of $150,000.

If a 401(k) plan is found to be top heavy, the employer will be ordered to contribute a minimum of 3 percent of compensation for the lower paid employees, whether or not the employees elected to participate. In addition, the plan will be subject to accelerated vesting (3-year or 2-to-6-year graded).

CONTRIBUTIONS

Once a 401(k) plan satisfies the minimum coverage and participation rules, the next step is to ensure that plan contributions and benefits do not discriminate in favor of employees who are officers, shareholders or highly compensated. This is accomplished by satisfying certain contribution and benefit limits. Plans that do not comply with these limits will not qualify for favorable tax treatment.

Elective Deferral Limit

Elective deferrals are the amounts an employee elects to contribute to a qualified plan that can be excluded from income in the year contributed. The limit on elective deferrals to a 401(k) plan is $7,000 per year adjusted annually for cost-of-living increases. (For 1996 and 1997, the deferral limit was $9,500. Because the limit is only adjusted for inflation in increments of $500, it will remain unchanged until total inflation adjustments reach $500 or more.) If the limitation is exceeded, the excess must be reported as taxable income.

The $7,000 adjusted limit applies on a per taxpayer basis so that the participant cannot defer more than $7,000 adjusted per year under all qualified plans in which he or she participates. If this limit is exceeded by deferrals to a plan, the plan must return the excess to the employee by April 15 of the following year to avoid a double taxation of the excess. That is, these excess deferrals are not included in the cost basis of plan distributions; thus these amounts will be taxed as income now, and then taxed again when they are distributed in the future.

Plan Limits on Contributions

The Code provides plan limits on the amount of contribution that can be made on behalf of an employee-participant. As a general rule, a plan cannot provide for annual contributions of more than 25 percent of compensation or $30,000, whichever is less. For purposes of this rule, only the first $150,000 of compensation may be taken into account. If an employer maintains more than one defined contribution plan, the limitation applies to the plans as a group, not separately. For example, suppose an employer maintains both a 401(k) profit-sharing plan and a money purchase pension plan. If an employee who has compensation of $80,000 participates in both, then the total annual additions to the two plans on behalf of that employee may not exceed $20,000 (which is the lesser of $30,000 or 25 percent of compensation). The employer may not contribute $20,000 to each of the two defined contribution plans. The same would be true if the employer had two 401(k) plans.

Highly Compensated Employee Limit

Under the 401(k) rules, a highly compensated employee's elective deferrals are restricted not only by the $7,000 indexed limit but also by special nondiscrimination rules. Since plans with 401(k) provisions could be used disproportionately by highly compensated employees and owners (who have more money to defer), special rules apply to ensure that the level of deferrals made by such employees are not disproportionate to deferrals made by rank-and-file employees.

To meet this requirement, the plan must satisfy one of two *actual deferral percentage (ADP)* tests, described below, or meet the requirements for a SIMPLE 401(k) plan (see Chapter 10). After 1998, an alternative "safe harbor" test can be used.

Actual Deferral Percentage Test

The actual deferral percentage, or ADP, test will be satisfied if:

- the percentage of actual deferrals by highly compensated employees for the plan year does not exceed the percentage of actual deferrals of all other eligible employees for the preceding year multiplied by 1.25; or

- the actual deferral percentage of highly compensated employees for the plan year is not more than 2 percentage points higher than the ADP of all other eligible employees for the preceding year *and* is not more than 2 times the percentage of actual deferrals of all other employees for the preceding year.

The actual deferral percentages for a group (highly compensated or nonhighly compensated) is the *average* of ratios (calculated separately for each employee) of elective contributions to compensation. (For the definition of *highly compensated employee,* see earlier discussion under "Nondiscrimination and Coverage Requirements.") For example, if an employee's compensation is $50,000 and his elective deferral is $5,000, the deferral percentage for that employee is 10 percent. If there are three nonhighly compensated employees and their individual deferral percentages last year were 10 percent, 8 percent and 6 percent, the ADP for that group is 8 percent [(.10 + .08 + .06) ÷ 3]. Consequently, 8 percent is the figure against which the ADP for the highly compensated group will be measured.

For the first year a plan is in existence, the ADP for nonhighly compensated employees for the preceding year will automatically be deemed to be 3 percent.

Alternative Safe Harbor Test

As of 1999, a 401(k) plan will be able to use an alternative "safe harbor" test to determine whether it meets the nondiscrimination requirements. The safe harbor test requires that (1) each eligible employee be given written notice of his or her rights under the plan and (2) the plan must meet one of two contribution requirements:

- Each nonhighly compensated employee who participates must receive *matching contributions* equal to (a) 100 percent of his or her elective contributions up to 3 percent of compensation *plus* (b) 50 percent of his or her elective contributions that exceed 3 percent of compensation, up to 5 percent of compensation. Some variations of this formula will be allowed, so long as the resulting amounts are essentially the same as under these percentages.

- Each nonhighly compensated employee eligible to participate—not merely those who make elective contributions—must receive a *nonelective contribution* from the employer equal to at least 3 percent of compensation.

Under either of these two approaches, contributions must be fully vested and subject to the withdrawal restrictions applicable to 401(k) plans.

Excess Contributions

Contributions in excess of the individual ceiling on elective deferrals are *excess deferrals.* Excess deferrals are not excludable from the employee's income and should be returned to the employee (along with any earnings the excess deferral generated). Contributions in excess of the maximum amount allowed under the ADP for highly compensated employees are *excess contributions.* They, too, are taxable to the employee. Excess contributions can—and should—be "corrected" by distributing the excess amounts (and any earnings) to the highly compensated employee. If the correction is not made or the excess is not distributed within 2½ months after the end of the plan year, the employer will be subject to a 10 percent excise tax. Excess contributions can be "recharacterized" as after-tax employee contributions if the plan allows such contributions.

Employer Matching Contributions

The employer may, if it wants, make "matching contributions" of a given percentage of part or all of employee deferrals. This encourages lower paid employees to make elective deferrals, which raises the ADP test for highly compensated employees and enables those highly compensated employees to make larger elective deferrals (as well as to receive matching contributions themselves). Matching contributions are subject to the actual contribution percentage test, which is similar to the ADP test.

Social Security

Before 1984, the employee's elective deferrals to a 401(k) plan were not subject to Social Security taxes. Although this resulted in less immediate tax, the long-term effect was to reduce the participant's Social Security retirement benefit because the amount deferred did not appear on Social Security records as earnings. Currently, employee contributions are subject to both Social Security (FICA) and federal unemployment (FUTA) taxes.

ILL. 3.2 ■ Comparison of Matching Contributions, Grouped by Plan Offerings

Companies that offer a defined benefit pension plan and a 401(k) plan generally match more per dollar than companies that provide a 401(k) plan exclusively.

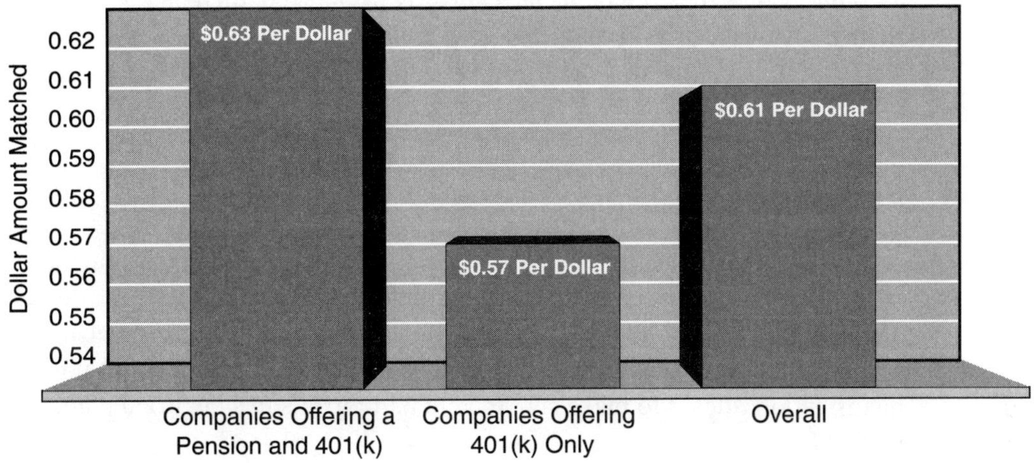

Source: BUCK CONSULTANTS

Design Considerations

A 401(k) plan's primary reason for existence is to allow employees a tax-advantaged way to save money for retirement. Although this advantage potentially benefits employees at all income levels, saving taxes likely will be of more interest to those that the tax code defines as highly compensated.

The highly compensated, however, are affected by the number of lower paid employees who decide to participate and the percentage of income they elect to defer. A plan will not qualify unless participation by eligible employees, both the highly and the nonhighly compensated, meets the minimum participation standards, as described above. Also, the percentage of income that the highly compensated can elect to defer depends on the deferral percentages of the other employees under the special nondiscrimination rules. Therefore, if a plan is to be of significant benefit to the highly compensated, then the lower paid workers must be persuaded not only to join the plan but also to contribute a reasonably high percentage of income.

Because the tax savings advantage may not be sufficient to convince nonhighly paid employees to participate and to contribute to a great enough extent, the plan's design could offer additional incentives. One way to enhance the appeal of the plan is to offer a life insurance purchase option. This will be discussed later. Another common way to increase plan participation by the rank-and-file is to provide for employer matching contributions. For example, the plan might provide that the employer will contribute one dollar for every dollar the employee contributes through salary reduction, up to 3 percent of salary, and $0.50 for every dollar above this, up to 5 percent of salary. Or, a plan may call for employer contributions of $0.50 for every dollar of salary reduction, up to 6 percent of salary. The variations are endless.

A plan also may permit employees to make after-tax contributions to their 401(k) accounts. Since these amounts have already been taxed, there is no immediate tax savings. However, the earnings do grow on a tax-deferred basis.

SUMMARY

A plan is not qualified unless it satisfies certain qualification requirements and contribution rules. Although compliance with these complicated tests is often onerous and time consuming, employers are willing to undertake the effort because of the favorable tax treatment received by qualified plans. And the main purpose of the qualification rules is to make sure that all participants in a qualified plan are treated equitably.

CHAPTER 3 QUESTIONS FOR REVIEW

1. A 401(k) arrangement whereby the employee makes all of the contributions to his or her account through salary reduction is called a

   A. cash option plan
   B. savings plan
   C. top-heavy plan
   D. 403(b) plan

2. Under a three-to-seven vesting schedule, a participant must be 20 percent vested after how many years of service?

   A. One year
   B. Three years
   C. Five years
   D. Seven years

3. The annual adjusted limit on elective deferrals to a 401(k) plan is

   A. $2,000
   B. $5,000
   C. $7,000
   D. $30,000

4. Which of the following employees would fall within the definition of a highly compensated employee?

   A. Employee who was a 1 percent owner during the previous year
   B. Employee who was an officer of the company
   C. Employee who was a 5 percent owner during the current or previous year
   D. Employee who received compensation in excess of $30,000 in the current year

5. Employee contributions to a 401(k) plan are subject to

   A. Social Security taxes only
   B. federal unemployment taxes only
   C. neither Social Security taxes nor federal unemployment taxes
   D. both Social Security taxes and federal unemployment taxes

4

Distributions

A distribution from a qualified plan can generally be defined as any removal or withdrawal of funds from the plan. In the case of distributions from a 401(k) plan, considerable flexibility is available. However, to maintain qualified plan status, 401(k) distribution provisions must satisfy Code requirements.

DISTRIBUTIONS IN GENERAL

Distributions from a 401(k) plan occur for a variety of reasons, of which retirement is usually seen as the primary reason. However, distributions are taken on many other occasions. Following are typical events that would trigger a distribution:

- attainment of age 59½
- death
- disability
- separation from service
- plan termination, sale of corporate assets and/or sale of corporate subsidiary
- hardship
- reaching age 70½ or retirement

Attainment of Age 59½, Death or Disability

The provision allowing distributions when a participant has reached age 59½ applies only to profit-sharing and stock bonus plans. It would not, for example, allow a participant to receive funds from a 401(k) that is part of a money purchase pension plan.

If an employee dies while still a participant in the plan, then the value of the deceased's account will go to his or her beneficiary. The account's value can be paid out to the beneficiary as either an annuity or in a lump sum.

Disability is defined as being unable to engage in any substantial gainful activity by reason of a medically determinable physical or mental impairment that can be expected to result in death or to last a long, indefinite period.

There is a 10 percent penalty tax for early withdrawals. However, this does not apply to distributions because of attainment of age 59½, death or disability. So, withdrawals for any of these reasons means that the employee or beneficiary would only have to pay the regular income tax due.

Separation from Service

This provision covers the situations where the employee quits or is fired by the employer. To qualify as a separation from service, the employee's break with the employer must be total. The ex-employee cannot be associated with the former employer in any way. For example, leaving the parent corporation to work for a subsidiary will not qualify as a separation from service.

Plan Termination and Sale of Corporate Assets or Subsidiary

There are three situations recognized by the Code when the actions of the employer rather than the employee will cause a distribution to take place. The first is the termination of the plan without the establishment of a successor plan. The second involves the sale by a corporation of substantially all of the assets used by the company in a trade or business. The provision applies to an employee who continues employment with the corporation that acquires the assets. The third new provision applies to an employee who continues employment with a subsidiary after its sale by a corporation.

Hardship Withdrawals

Hardship withdrawals under 401(k) plans and other similar cash or deferred arrangements (CODAs) are often used to provide access to needed cash. A hardship withdrawal is permitted only if:

- the participant has an *immediate and heavy financial need;*
- no other resources are available to meet the need;
- the distribution is limited to the amount required to relieve the hardship; and
- the withdrawal does not exceed the amount the participant has electively contributed to the plan.

ILL. 4.1 ■ *Hardship Withdrawals*

Approximately 92 percent of the organizations that sponsor a 401(k) plan permit hardship withdrawals. Respondents mentioned the following circumstances for allowing hardship withdrawals:

- payment of (uncovered) medical expenses (98 percent)
- purchase of a principal residence (94 percent)
- payment of post-secondary education tuition (92 percent)
- prevention of the eviction from, or foreclosure on, an employee's principal residence (89 percent)
- payment of funeral expenses (22 percent)

Plan sponsors can typically use one of two methods to determine financial hardship.

Under the first method, the employee must provide a signed statement that the financial need cannot be satisfied through reimbursement or compensation by insurance, reasonable liquidation of employee's assets, the suspension of elective or after-tax contributions to the plan, other distributions or nontaxable loans from employer-provided plans or loans from commercial lenders on reasonable commercial terms.

- or -

Under the second method, the employee is not required to provide a signed statement concerning the lack of financial resources. However, the hardship withdrawal may be granted only if all of the following conditions are met:

a. The amount of the requested hardship withdrawal does not exceed the amount necessary to meet the immediate and heavy financial need.

b. The employee has received all other distributions and all nontaxable loans under the plan.

c. The employee's elective deferrals and after-tax contributions under all plans are suspended for at least 12 months after the hardship withdrawal distribution.

d. After the 12-month suspension, the employee's maximum annual deferral in the calendar year of resumption will be reduced by the amount of elective deferrals made in the calendar year that the hardship withdrawal was made.

Source: BUCK CONSULTANTS

Whether an immediate and heavy financial need exists is based on the facts and circumstances of the individual case. Medical expenses, the down payment on a principal home, college tuition and funds needed to forestall foreclosure would likely satisfy the financial need requirement.

Hardship withdrawals are considered taxable income and if taken before age 59½, are subject to the 10 percent early distribution penalty. Also, a participant who receives a hardship withdrawal is prohibited from making any contributions to the 401(k) plan for at least 12 months after the withdrawal.

Reaching Age 70½ or Retirement

Distributions from a 401(k) plan must begin by the *later of:*

- age 70½ or
- retirement

However, the first distribution may be delayed until April 1 of the year after the year the participant turns 70½ or retires. This date is known as the "required distribution date." After the first distribution, all subsequent distributions must be taken by December 31 of each calendar year. Failure to take a required distribution results in a penalty tax equal to 50 percent of the difference between the amount that should have been taken and the amount actually taken.

■ DISTRIBUTIONS BY AGE

In order to determine the treatment of a distribution, it is important to know the age of the plan participant. When considering a participant's age, distributions are viewed as falling into one of three categories:

1. pre-age 59½
2. age 59½ to age 70½
3. post-age 70½

Pre-Age 59½

Distributions from a qualified or individual retirement plan are generally not allowed before the participant or owner reaches the age of 59½. Distributions taken before this age are considered "early" or "premature." Premature distributions are subject to a 10 percent penalty tax unless the distribution qualifies as an exception to the penalty. The penalty tax applies in addition to applicable income taxes.

Age 59½ to Age 70½

Between the ages of 59½ and 70½ distributions may be taken but are not required to be taken. Plan participants need only comply with the rules of the employer's plan.

Post-Age 70½

As noted above, qualified plan distributions must begin by the later of (1) age 70½ or (2) retirement.

PREMATURE DISTRIBUTIONS

Any distribution received before age 59½ is considered a premature distribution subject to a 10 percent penalty tax under IRC §72(t). The penalty is applied to the portion of the distribution that is includable in income.

Exceptions to the 10 Percent Premature Distribution Penalty

There are exceptions to the 10 percent penalty tax. Even if a participant is below age 59½, the penalty tax will not apply if the distribution occurs under any of the following circumstances:

- it is made because of the employee's death or disability;
- it is made to an employee who has reached age 55, separated from service and has met the early retirement requirements of the plan;
- it is made pursuant to a qualified domestic relations order;
- it is made to pay medical expenses that exceed 7.5 percent of adjusted gross income;
- it is part of a scheduled series of substantially equal periodic payments over the participant's life or the joint lives of the participant and beneficiary; or
- it is made to reduce or correct excess contributions or deferrals.

TAXATION OF DISTRIBUTIONS

General Rule

Generally, amounts that were not previously taxed are taxable as ordinary income when distributed from a 401(k). If benefits are received in the form of installment or annuity payments and if no after-tax contributions were made to the plan, then the entire amount of each payment is taxable. If the employee has a *cost basis* in the account, then part of each payment represents a return of previously taxed amounts and is not taxable again. The employee's cost basis in the account equals the value of any after-tax contributions he or she made to the 401(k) plan and, if the plan contains life insurance, the total of P.S. 58 costs of the insurance.

How much is taxable is determined by applying an *exclusion ratio*. This is the ratio that the employee's cost basis represents to the total expected return. The total return is based upon the employee's life expectancy and the payout terms. For example, if the employee's cost basis is $5,000 and the total expected return is $100,000, then 1/20th ($5,000 ÷ $100,000) of each payment represents a return of previously taxed income and that portion is received tax free. However, once a participant has received nontaxable income equal to the cost basis, then the total amount of future payments is taxable.

Lump-Sum Distributions

Individuals who receive their benefits in a lump sum are able to take advantage of a special averaging technique to reduce tax liability. A *lump-sum distribution* is one that is received within one taxable year and represents the employee's entire account balance. In addition, the distribution must be received by reason of the employee's death, disability, attainment of age 59½ or because of the employee's separation from service. (The disability requirement applies only to self-employed individuals; the separation from service requirement applies only to common-law employees and not to the self-employed.) Also, for a distribution to be treated as a lump-sum distribution, the employee must have been a plan participant for five or more years before the year of the distribution.

Lump-sum distributions may be eligible for forward averaging tax treatment. Forward averaging treats the distribution as if it were received over a number of years instead of in a single year, which reduces the tax liability. Although the tax is still paid, at once, for the year of distribution, the amount of tax is less than if forward averaging were not used. To be eligible for forward averaging:

- the distribution must qualify for lump-sum treatment;
- the participant must be over the age of 59½ when the distribution is received; and

- the participant must elect forward averaging treatment on all lump-sum distributions received during a single year.

Forward averaging is available for qualifying lump-sum distributions under the following rules:

- Participants who were 50 before January 1, 1986, can (a) choose to 10-year average using 1986 tax rates or (b) elect capital gains treatment at a 20 percent long-term capital gains rate for the pre-1974 portion of the distribution.

- Participants not 50 before January 1, 1986, may elect five-year averaging through tax years up to December 31, 1999.

■ ROLLOVERS

A rollover is a tax-free transfer of money or property distributed from a qualified plan, 401(k) plan, IRA or SEP to another plan or plans. Rollovers allow plan participants to take a distribution—a transaction that is usually taxable—and deposit it in another plan without taxes or penalties.

Types of Rollovers

There are generally two types of rollovers:

1. direct rollovers

2. indirect rollovers

Under a direct rollover the funds are sent by the trustee of the distributing plan directly to the trustee of the receiving plan. The plan participant is not involved in the transaction except to initiate it. In the case of an indirect rollover, the plan participant personally receives the funds from the distributing plan and turns them over to the trustee of the receiving plan.

Timing

Rollovers must be completed within 60 days. This means a plan participant who receives plan benefits has 60 calendar days to roll the funds over to a new plan.

Required Minimum Distributions

A required minimum distribution may not be rolled over. Rollovers, however, can be made during years in which required minimum distributions must be taken, as long as the required amount is in fact distributed.

Eligible Rollover Amount

There is no limit on the amount in a plan that may be rolled over. None of the following amounts, however, are eligible for rollover treatment:

- a distribution that is part of a series of substantially equal payments continuing over the life expectancy of the participant, the joint life expectancy of the participant and his or her beneficiary or a period of 10 years or more;
- a distribution that is not includable in the participant's taxable income; or
- a distribution made to correct an excess contribution or excess deferral.

Twenty Percent Withholding

For rollovers from qualified plans, there is a mandatory 20 percent withholding if the participant takes receipt of the funds. This means 20 percent of the rollover will be withheld by the distributing trustee as assumed federal income tax before it is distributed to the participant. This rule applies only to rollovers from qualified plans—not from IRAs—and only when the distribution is made to the participant. A participant may make up the 20 percent withheld on the rollover and claim a refund of that amount on his or her tax return. In cases where the participant fails to make up the 20 percent, a taxable distribution of the full 20 percent is deemed to be made. The tax may also include a penalty of 10 percent if the participant is under 59½.

Partial Distributions

If the amount received represents only a partial distribution, it may be transferred only to an IRA. A partial distribution is one that represents at least 50 percent of the employee's account balance and that otherwise meets the tests in the definition of a lump-sum distribution received within one year and payable on account of the employee's attainment of age 59½, etc.

PENALTY TAXES

A number of penalty taxes may apply to distributions from 401(k) plans. Congress included these taxes as a way either to ensure that 401(k)s and other qualified plans were used primarily as retirement plans, and not simply as tax shelters, or to penalize benefit distributions from such tax-favored retirement plans that it viewed as excess.

Ten Percent Early Withdrawal Tax

As noted above, a 10 percent tax is imposed on early withdrawals from a qualified plan. For example, if a taxpayer receives an early taxable distribution of $120,000, then there is a penalty tax of $12,000 due in addition to the regular income tax liability, unless the distribution falls within one of the exceptions previously discussed.

Fifty Percent Penalty Tax

As noted above, distributions from a 401(k) plan must begin no later than April 1 of the year after the year the participant turns 70½ or retires.

If distributions in a year fall below the *minimum distribution amount,* then a 50 percent penalty tax is imposed on the difference between the required minimum distribution and the amount distributed. The minimum distribution amount basically equals the account balance divided by the recipient's life expectancy, or joint life expectancy of the participant and beneficiary, based on attained age.

In determining the minimum distribution allowance (MDA) for a year, the account balance used is the balance at the end of the previous year and the life expectancy is based on the participant's age at the end of the year for which the MDA is being calculated. For example, suppose the MDA for 1997 is being calculated. The account balance at the end of 1996 is $153,000, and the participant will be age 71 at the end of 1997. According to IRS tables, the life expectancy at age 71 is 15.3 years. So, the MDA for 1997 is $153,000/15.3 or $10,000. If the participant receives less than $10,000, then the 50 percent tax applies. If, for example, only $6,000 is received, the participant will owe a penalty tax of $2,000, or half of ($10,000 – $6,000).

Fifteen Percent Excise Tax

Until recently, a 15 percent excise tax was imposed on *excess distributions* from qualified retirement plans, including 401(k)s. The Small Business Act of 1996, however, has suspended the 15 percent excise tax on excess distributions until January 1, 2000. Prior to suspension of the tax, excess distributions were defined as the excess of the total amount of retirement distributions from all qualified plans during a year over $112,500. (This amount continues to be adjusted annually for inflation and was

$155,000 for 1996.) For example, if a participant received retirement distributions in 1996 of $175,000, then there was a 15 percent tax on the $20,000 in distributions in excess of the $155,000 limit.

However, the tax liability under the 15 percent tax was reduced by any penalty for early withdrawals that applied to the excess distribution. So, if the participant also owed a tax for early withdrawals on the $175,000 distribution, then the $3,000 due under the 15 percent excess distribution tax was reduced proportionally by the 10 percent early withdrawal tax applicable to that amount ($2,000). Thus, the participant owed a total penalty tax on the excess premature distribution of $18,500 [$17,500 + ($3,000 – $2,000)].

The following items were not taken into account when determining if excess distributions were received:

- any retirement distribution made because of the death of the participant (however, a 15 percent estate tax penalty does apply);
- any retirement distribution made under a qualified domestic relations order;
- any retirement distribution representing the employee's investment in the contract (cost basis); or
- any retirement distribution not included in gross income because of a rollover.

If the employee received a lump-sum distribution and elected income averaging, then the excess distribution limit applied separately to that amount and the limit was increased to five times the annual threshold amount ($775,000 in 1996).

The Grandfather Election

Individuals who had qualified plan assets of $562,500 or more as of August 1, 1986, had the opportunity to grandfather those amounts and shield them from the excess distribution tax. Consequently, if an individual received a distribution and part of it was attributable to benefits or values accrued as of August 1, 1986, he or she could elect to have no 15 percent tax imposed on any excess distributions coming from those benefits. However, the distribution attributable to those benefits would be taken into account in determining if excess distributions were received.

The ability to elect grandfathering of pre-August 1, 1986 retirement assets expired at the end of 1988.

■ SUMMARY

This chapter has covered the basics of distributions from 401(k) plans. As you can see, the applicability of the distribution rules depends on a number of factors—circumstance, type of plan, type of distribution and age of the participant. In many cases the rules and regulations governing distributions are complicated and the consequences of error are severe. Because distribution rules are confusing, it is important to have a good grasp of basic concepts and seek competent advice whenever questions arise.

■ CHAPTER 4 QUESTIONS FOR REVIEW

1. Distributions from a 401(k) plan must begin by the LATER of

   A. age 59½ or retirement
   B. age 60 or retirement
   C. age 70½ or retirement
   D. age 65 or retirement

2. A distribution received before age 59½ is considered a premature distribution subject to a penalty tax of what percentage?

   A. 25 percent
   B. 75 percent
   C. 15 percent
   D. 10 percent

3. Which of the following is NOT an exception to the premature distribution penalty tax?

   A. Distribution made to purchase a primary residence
   B. Distribution because of an employee's death or disability
   C. Distribution made pursuant to a qualified domestic relations order
   D. Distribution to pay medical expenses that exceed 7.5 percent of adjusted gross income

4. Which of the following is a tax-free transfer of money or property distributed from a qualified plan, 401(k) plan, IRA or SEP to another plan or plans?

   A. Required minimum distribution
   B. Premature distribution
   C. Hardship withdrawal
   D. Rollover

5. All of the following describe a lump-sum distribution EXCEPT

   A. it is received within one taxable year and represents the employee's entire account balance
   B. it is a tax-free transfer of money or property distributed from a qualified plan
   C. it must be received within one taxable year and represents the employee's entire account balance
   D. it may qualify for a special averaging technique to reduce tax liability

5

Plan Loans

A 401(k) plan often includes a provision that allows a participant to borrow against his or her account balance. Employees appreciate this feature because it allows them to dip into the money in the plan without incurring any income tax on the borrowed funds. A loan provision reassures plan participants that the money contributed to the plan is not beyond reach until retirement.

BASIC RULES GOVERNING PLAN LOANS

The basic tax rules governing 401(k) plan loans are that they must:

- be made in accordance with the specific loan provisions in the plan;
- be available to all participants on a reasonably equivalent basis;
- not be made available to highly compensated employees in an amount greater than that made available to other employees;
- bear a reasonable rate of interest;
- be adequately secured; and
- be repaid within five years.

ILL. 5.1 ■ Prevalence of 401(k) Loan Provisions

The prevalence of loan provisions in 401(k) plans has increased over the years.

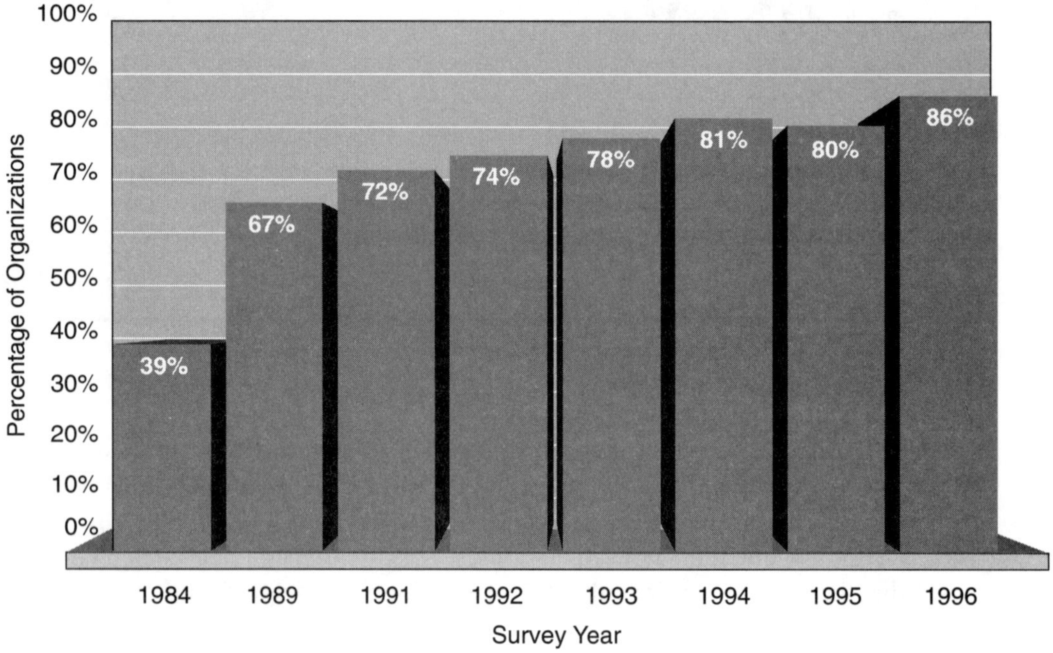

Source: BUCK CONSULTANTS

■ MAXIMUM LOAN AMOUNT

The maximum amount that a plan participant may borrow, when added to the participant's other outstanding loan balances from the plan, cannot exceed the lesser of:

- $50,000, reduced by the highest outstanding loan balance during the one-year period ending the day before the date on which the new loan is made less the outstanding balance on the day of the loan; or

- the greater of (a) one-half of the participant's vested account balance or (b) $10,000.

Let's consider each part of this limit.

As to the first part, suppose that an employee has a vested account balance of $120,000. He has withdrawn loan amounts previously and wants to take out a new loan. On the day of the new loan, there is no outstanding loan balance. However, the employee did have an outstanding plan loan during the one-year period ending on the day before the new loan date. The highest outstanding balance on this previous loan during that one-year period was $20,000. So, the $50,000 amount would be reduced by the excess of the highest outstanding balance during the year ($20,000) less the outstanding balance on the day of the new loan ($0). Therefore, the $50,000 part of the loan limit is reduced by $20,000 ($20,000 – $0) to $30,000.

The second part of the limit is determined by taking the larger of one-half of the vested account balance or $10,000. In this example the vested amount is $120,000. Since half of this is larger than $10,000, the second part of the limit is $60,000. Because the maximum loan is the lesser of the amounts determined under each part of the formula ($30,000 and $60,000), the maximum loan amount for the employee is $30,000, even though there was no loan outstanding on the day of the new loan.

Keep in mind that the new loan, when added to any outstanding loan, cannot exceed the amount determined under the above formula. Consider this situation: Vested account balance = $90,000; outstanding balance on day of new loan = $15,000; highest outstanding balance during year ending the day before the new loan date = $25,000. Under the formula, $40,000 is the lesser of (1) $40,000 ($50,000 – [$25,000 – $15,000]) or (2) $45,000 (the greater of [a] half of $90,000 or [b] $10,000). However, there is an outstanding balance of $15,000, so the maximum new loan that the employee can take out is $25,000 ($40,000 – $15,000).

■ TERM OF THE LOAN

Generally, loans must be repaid within five years. There is one significant exception to this repayment schedule. If a loan is used to acquire the principal residence of the plan participant, for his or her use only, the five-year rule does not apply. The loan agreement must also provide for substantially level amortization of the loan and at least quarterly payments.

Congress added the level amortization, quarterly payments requirement and the $50,000 limit in the loan formula because of what it saw as abuse of 401(k) loans. Under the prior rules, participants often were permitted to make only interest payments within the five years with a balloon payment at the end, only to take out a new loan. In effect, a participant was able to maintain a permanent outstanding loan. The legislators considered this inappropriate because the 401(k) plan was designed as a means of saving for retirement.

INTEREST

All qualified plan loans are required to carry a "reasonable rate" of interest. A reasonable rate is defined as one that is commensurate with commercial loan rates. Interest paid on plan loans is not deductible for tax purposes.

Interest paid on a plan loan is added to the participant's own account, but the interest does not increase his or her basis in the plan. That is, when the interest payments along with principal are received by the participant during a plan distribution (e.g., at retirement), the full amount of the interest received will be taxable. This is the case even if the interest was paid with nondeductible dollars. So, a participant could be taxed twice on the same interest payments.

Suppose that over the course of participation in a 401(k) plan an employee paid $10,000 in nondeductible interest on plan loans. The $10,000 was added to the employee's account but did not increase his or her cost basis. Assuming the employee has no cost basis in the account, every cent of the benefits received from the 401(k) plan, including the $10,000 paid with nondeductible or after-tax dollars, would be subject to regular income taxation.

EMPLOYEE DEPARTURE OR TERMINATION

Repayment in full of any outstanding loan balance is required if a participant leaves his or her employer. In cases where a participant defaults on a plan loan, the outstanding balance is treated as a taxable distribution. The 10 percent premature distribution penalty will apply if the participant is younger than 59½.

TAXATION

If a loan from a 401(k) plan does not meet the requirements outlined above, the loan is considered a plan distribution and is taxable as ordinary income. In addition, if the distribution is early, the 10 percent penalty tax also applies.

PLAN VARIATIONS

It is important to note that the loan rules concerning amounts and repayment schedules are imposed by the tax code. Nothing in the Code prohibits a 401(k) from having rules that are more restrictive than those discussed. For example, a plan might require repayment within four years or, because of the paperwork involved in a loan, it might set a minimum amount that can be borrowed. Of course, any provision could not discriminate in favor of the prohibited group.

ILL. 5.2 ■ *To Borrow or Not To Borrow*

According to recent studies conducted by employee benefit consulting firms, employers are increasingly making it easier for participants to borrow against their qualified plan funds. For example, approximately 80 percent of today's 401(k) plans include a loan provision, and many participants have taken advantage of it.

For many, the long-term consequences of borrowing against retirement funds may be negligible. A 35-year-old participant who borrows, say, $6,000 from his plan, pays it back in three years with interest, and continues to contribute to the plan, will probably wind up with a retirement fund only a few thousand dollars less than what it would have been if he hadn't taken out the loan. In this way, a qualified plan can serve as a source of needed funds.

However, participants should be aware of the potential danger of relying on loans from their qualified plans, especially if there is the possibility they may leave or be forced out of their jobs and be unable to repay the loan. Typical loan provisions require repayment in full of any outstanding loan balance if a participant leaves his or her employer; the repayment is usually deducted from the accrued balance in the plan. In addition, if a participant defaults on a plan loan, the outstanding balance will be treated as a taxable distribution, with the 10 percent penalty applying if the participant is younger than 59½.

■ SUMMARY

Loans are a popular 401(k) plan feature. From a participant's perspective, loans can provide access to funds prior to retirement at potentially lower interest rate than would be available from other lenders. Moreover, repayment through payroll deductions is convenient.

■ CHAPTER 5 QUESTIONS FOR REVIEW

1. As a general rule, loans from a 401(k) plan must be repaid within how many years?

    A. 5
    B. 10
    C. 15
    D. 20

2. Which of the following statements concerning the interest rate on a plan loan is NOT correct?

   A. All qualified plan loans are required to carry a "reasonable" rate of interest.
   B. A reasonable rate of interest is one that is commensurate with commercial loan rates.
   C. Interest paid on plan loans is deductible for tax purposes.
   D. Interest paid on a plan loan is added to the participant's own account, but does not increase his or her basis in the plan.

3. The amount of a plan loan is generally limited to the lesser of

   A. (1) $100,000 or (2) the greater of 75 percent of the participant's vested balance or $20,000
   B. (1) $250,000 or (2) the greater of 80 percent of the participant's vested balance or $30,000
   C. (1) $75,000 or (2) the greater of 25 percent of the participant's vested balance or $5,000
   D. (1) $50,000 or (2) the greater of 50 percent of the participant's vested balance or $10,000

4. Which of the following statements is NOT correct concerning plan loans?

   A. Loans to highly compensated employees may be made available in an amount greater than that made available to other employees.
   B. Loans must be made in accordance with specific loan provisions in the plan.
   C. Loans must be adequately secure.
   D. Loans must be made available to all participants on a reasonable equivalent basis.

5. Which of the following is an exception to the five-year repayment requirement?

   A. Loans used to pay college tuition
   B. Loans made for the purchase of a principal residence
   C. Loans used for adoption expenses
   D. Loans used to pay medical expenses

6

Plan Investment Requirements

Providing a selection of investment options is an integral part of 401(k) plan design. This allows plan participants to allocate plan contributions among those investments most suitable to their retirement and financial needs. The type and number of investment alternatives is not a plan qualification requirement regulated by the Tax Code. However, virtually all 401(k) plans choose to voluntarily comply with the provisions of ERISA §404(c) which require (1) prudence in managing the plan assets and (2) adequate portfolio diversification. By satisfying §404(c) the plan will obtain relief from certain fiduciary rules when participants incur financial loss as a result of their own investment decisions.

SECTION 404(c) OVERVIEW

Compliance with the Department of Labor regulations under ERISA §404(c) is not mandatory and is not a prerequisite to qualified plan status. However, a majority of 401(k) plans voluntarily satisfy ERISA §404(c) conditions for the express purpose of obtaining limited relief from certain fiduciary rules in the event of a participant's loss of investment assets. The effect of §404(c) relief is two-part:

1. A plan participant will not be treated as a fiduciary because of his or her exercise of control over assets in his or her account.

2. No other plan fiduciaries will be liable for losses stemming from a participant's exercise of control.

ILL. 6.1 ■ ERISA §404(c) Plan Illustration

An ERISA §404(c) plan is an individual account plan that focuses on the opportunity for a participant to exercise control over assets in his or her individual account.

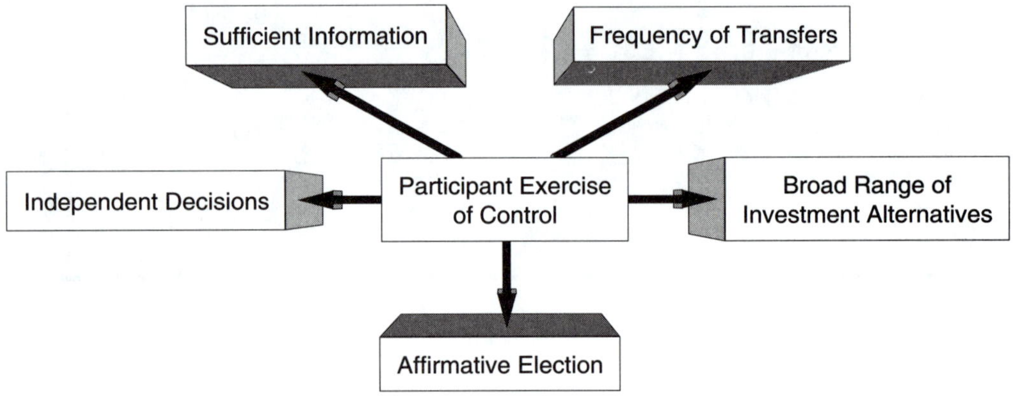

Note that protection under §404(c) is transactional in nature. The plan as a whole is not protected but rather relief is afforded on a case-by-case basis.

SECTION 404(c) REQUIREMENTS

A 401(k) plan that chooses to comply with ERISA §404(c) must provide individual accounts for each participant and give participants the ability to exercise independent control over assets in his or her account. To receive §404(c) protection, a 401(k) plan must also satisfy the following requirements:

- Plan participants must have access to a broad range of investment alternatives that include at least three core diversified options.
- Plan participants must have the ability to transfer assets among investment options at least quarterly.
- To permit informed decision making, sufficient investment information must be provided on all investment options.

ILL. 6.2 ■ *ERISA §404(c) Regulations*

Eighty-three percent of the plan sponsors report that they are in compliance with the ERISA §404(c) regulations. Of those plan sponsors that are not in compliance with these regulations, 28 percent attributed noncompliance to issues surrounding participant education or communication.

Broad Range of Investment Alternatives

The §404(c) requirement that a participant be offered a broad range of investment alternatives is satisfied if the plan offers at least three categories of investment, or "core" alternatives, each of which must be diversified and have materially different risk and return characteristics. The three core investment alternatives offered must allow the participant to achieve a portfolio with aggregate risk and return characteristics within an acceptable range for that individual. Also, investment choices available must give participants the opportunity to materially affect the degree of risk and potential returns as well as diversify accounts to minimize risk of large losses.

Employer securities, because they lack diversification, cannot qualify as a core alternative. However, employer securities as well as additional investment vehicles not meeting the core alternatives requirement, may be offered as supplemental investment options. If offered as a noncore alternative, employer securities must satisfy the following conditions:

- The securities must be qualifying securities as defined by ERISA.
- The securities must be stock.
- The securities must be publicly traded on a national exchange or other generally recognized market.
- The securities must be traded with sufficient frequency and in a volume that buy or sell directions can be responded to promptly.
- Information provided to shareholders must also be provided to plan participants.
- Voting and similar rights must be passed through to plan participants.
- Transactions involving the securities must be handled in a confidential manner and monitored by a designated or, if necessary, independent fiduciary.

ILL. 6.3 ■ Types of Funds Offered by 401(k) Plans, by Major Category

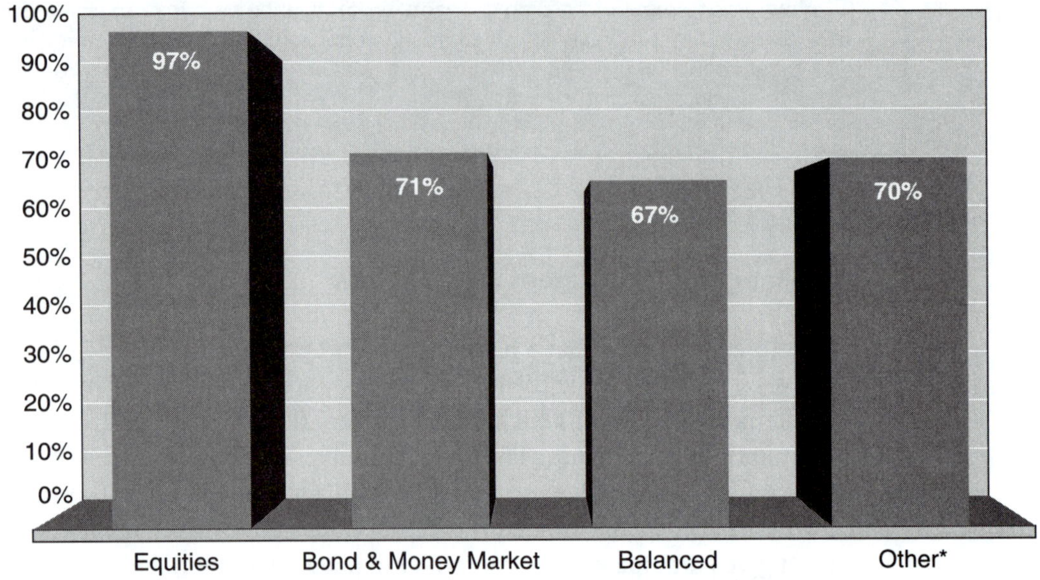

* Includes Stable Value Funds, Mutual Fund Windows and Self Directed Brokerage Accounts

Source: BUCK CONSULTANTS

Common Core Investment Options

No specific categories of investments are required to be included a core investment options. But given the broad diversification requirement and the small size of individual participant accounts, plans generally need to offer core alternatives that are "look through" investment vehicles, such as mutual funds and guaranteed investment contracts. This allows diversification requirements to be met based on the underlying assets of a pooled fund. Individual investment vehicles may be offered as additional options to the core alternatives.

Common core investment options include:

- fixed income contracts
- mutual funds
- annuities

An option that is often offered as a supplement to the core investment vehicles is life insurance. Each of the common core investment options as well as life insurance is discussed below.

Fixed Income Contract. One core option often available to participants is to deposit contributions with a bank or savings and loan. The plan administrator might be able to contract for a higher interest rate for the plan's funds than an individual depositor could receive for personal savings.

Another fixed income option is for the plan to enter into a guaranteed investment contract with an insurance company. Under this type of agreement, the insurer guarantees the plan a specified rate of return on the investment. This is a conservative investment for the plan since the insurer assumes the investment risks on the plan contributions.

Mutual Fund. As a core alternative, mutual funds provide the plan designer with a broad selection of fund types from which to choose. Mutual funds can be classified not only by the type of investment (stocks vs. bonds, for example) but also by investment philosophy (growth vs. growth and income). Since there are so many different types of funds, a 401(k) plan often will offer more than one mutual fund as an investment option. A plan commonly will include both a stock or equity fund and a bond fund. But whichever type of fund is chosen, a mutual fund offers investors a number of advantages, including professional management, diversification of investments and a ready market for the investment.

Annuity. A 401(k) may offer annuities as one of the core investment options. If this option is chosen, the plan designer must decide whether to offer fixed, variable or both annuity types. Under the fixed annuity, the annuitant is guaranteed a specified number of dollars each payout period. With a variable annuity, the periodic payment amount is based on the performance of the underlying investments. Between the two types, then, the fixed annuity would be the choice of a plan designer or plan participant interested in a more conservative investment for contributions.

Life Insurance. Life insurance is frequently offered as a supplement to core investment options. Although this option is covered in more detail in the following sections, it should be pointed out now that including life insurance as an option not only provides employees with a tax-advantaged way to purchase needed life insurance protection but also increase participation in the 401(k).

Keep in mind that the investment options discussed above are among the most common ones in 401(k) plans; they are certainly not the only ones. Other types of investments often found in 401(k) plans include corporate stock, even the employer's stock, bonds and deposit administration contracts.

Incidental Test. If life insurance is included as one of the options under the plan, the tax code requires that the cost of the insurance be *incidental*. Generally, if the cost of providing current life and health insurance benefits is less than 25 percent of the cost of providing all benefits under the plan, the incidental limitation is satisfied. The cost of term insurance is considered incidental if no more than 25 percent of the funds allocated to a participant's account is used to purchase the insurance. In the case of whole life coverage, the insurance is incidental if the premiums do not exceed 50 percent of the plan contributions. Universal and variable life insurance are subject to the 25 percent test.

P.S. 58 Cost. Although the employee's elective deferrals and employer contributions generally are not included in income, part of the cost of life insurance purchased under a 401(k) plan is taxable to the employee. This small taxable amount is determined using the IRS P.S. 58 rates or, if lower, the insurer's annual renewable term rates.

Benefits of Life Insurance. When life insurance is included as one of the investment options, it can offer substantial benefits to all interested parties. Many lower paid workers are underinsured, so the addition of life insurance to the plan allows these employees to buy coverage with mostly pretax dollars. Life insurance can also serve as a way to complete the insured's retirement savings program should he or she die while still actively employed.

A life insurance option also tends to increase participation of the nonhighly compensated employees. This increased participation benefits the highly compensated by making the 401(k) plan less likely to fail to meet the nondiscrimination requirements.

Finally, life insurance in a 401(k) presents the agent/planner with additional sales opportunities. Although the amount of coverage that a typical worker might buy may be relatively small, when this amount is multiplied by the number of plan participants, the potential sales amount jumps significantly.

Exercise of Investment Control

Section 404(c) requires that a participant have the ability to exercise control over his or her plan assets. Both the *opportunity* to exercise control and the *actual* exercise of control is assessed. The *opportunity* to exercise control exists if the participant has:

- sufficient information to make informed investment decisions
- a reasonable opportunity to give investment instructions
- his or her investment instructions carried out by the plan fiduciary

A participant's *actual* exercise of control is assessed based on his or her independent affirmatively elected control over plan assets.

Participant Investment Instructions

Under §404(c) participants must have the ability to give investment instructions—both written and oral—to an identified fiduciary and obtain written confirmation within a reasonable period of time upon request. Written procedures for giving investment instructions must be made available to all plan participants.

Refusal to follow a participant's investment instructions is allowed if the transaction would:

- violate the terms of the plan;
- cause plan assets to be maintained outside the jurisdiction of the federal courts;
- jeopardize the plan's tax-qualified status;
- result in a loss in excess of the participant's account balance;
- result in a transaction prohibited under ERISA or the Internal Revenue Code; or
- generate taxable income to the plan.

Frequency of Transfers

Section 404(c) requires that plan participants be able to reallocate plan assets with the frequency necessitated by the volatility of the core investment options. At a minimum, transfers must be allowed at least once every three months.

Plan Information Requirement

As a condition of §404(c) compliance, the plan fiduciary must provide two categories of information to plan participants:

1. information furnished automatically to all plan participants
2. information furnished only upon request

The following information must be provided automatically to all plan participants:

- notice that plan fiduciaries may not be liable for account losses resulting from participant investment instructions;

ILL 6.4 ■ *Permitted Frequency for Changing Investment Elections*

Plan participants are typically able to change investment elections for current contributions and existing account balances with greater frequency than in the past.

In 1989, only 4 percent of the plan sponsors permitted changes of investment elections for future contributions every pay period. Today, 49 percent permit changes every pay period. A similar trend exists with respect to the frequency with which participants are permitted to change investment elections for existing account balances. In 1989, only 4 percent of the plan sponsors permitted plan participants to change existing investment elections on a daily basis, as compared to 53 percent today.

Source: BUCK CONSULTANTS

- a description of each investment alternative available under the plan and the objectives and risk and return characteristics of each alternative;
- identification of all investment managers, if any;
- an explanation of how and when investment instructions may be given, including any restrictions and limitations on transfers;
- any transaction fees or other expenses that may be charged against plan account balances;
- the name, address and phone number of the plan fiduciary;
- confidentiality provisions for employer stock transactions;
- the prospectuses for all investment options for which prospectuses are required; and
- all proxy materials relating to plan investment options.

The following information must be made available to plan participants upon request:

- annual plan operating expenses;
- copies of financial statements relating to plan investment options;

- information on assets that comprise the portfolio of each investment alternative;
- investment performance information on each plan investment option; and
- information on the value of shares of an investment in their own account.

SUMMARY

The decision of whether to comply with ERISA §404(c) must be based on a constructive review of plan structures and operations. Virtually all 401(k) plans, however, choose to comply with §404(c) standards. This effectively places the investment risk for 401(k) funds with the plan participant. As a result, it is important that participants have a choice of investment funds that meet their needs and levels of risk tolerance.

CHAPTER 6 QUESTIONS FOR REVIEW

1. The provisions of which of the following allow a 401(k) plan to obtain relief from certain fiduciary rules when a plan participant incurs financial loss as a result of investment decisions?

   A. I.R.C. §401(a)
   B. ERISA §404(c)
   C. I.R.C. §415(c)
   D. ERISA §401(a)

2. Which of the following is NOT required under ERISA §404(c)?

   A. Individual accounts must be provided for each plan participant.
   B. Plan participants must have access to a broad range of investment alternatives.
   C. Each plan participant must have the ability to exercise independent control over assets in his or her account.
   D. All plan participants must have been employed by the plan sponsor for a minimum of three years.

3. Which of the following is NOT a common core investment option under ERISA §404(c)?

   A. Fixed income contracts
   B. Mutual funds
   C. Annuities
   D. Futures contracts

4. Under ERISA §404(c), plan participants must be able to reallocate plan assets

   A. once every three months
   B. annually
   C. daily
   D. once every week

5. Under ERISA §404(c), plan participants must have the ability to give investment instructions using which of the following methods?

   A. Written communication
   B. Oral communication
   C. Both written and oral communication
   D. Plan participants are not allowed to give investment instructions.

7
Marketing 401(k) Plans

Now that you understand the basics of a 401(k) plan and the requirements in plan designs, you are ready for your first 401(k) client. But where is the client? As this chapter unfolds, you will be able to identify prospects who will become your clients from sources that may surprise you. 401(k) plan presentations often require more than one interview. Do not be discouraged by this. When your prospect becomes your client, you will find many other sales will result.

EVALUATING THE 401(k) MARKET

One of the common fears when entering a new market is that there won't be any good prospects. A way to overcome this doubt about the market for 401(k) plans is to ask the following questions:

- Approximately how many businesses are there in my marketing area?
- How many of the business owners want to retain and recruit quality employees?
- How many of the business owners would be interested in a low-cost way to provide a fringe benefit that helps accomplish that goal?
- How many of the business owners have employees who would be interested in a way to save pretax income in a tax-advantaged account?

If a business owner would be interested in those benefits, then that owner is a prospect for a 401(k) plan. The size of the business doesn't matter. There is no minimum

> • Opportunities abound in the 401(k) marketplace, especially for small to mid-size companies.
>
> • Smart employers are re-evaluating regularly their choice of 401(k) providers.

size for establishing a 401(k) plan. In fact, small and midsize businesses might be better prospects than larger ones since they would be less likely to have a comprehensive fringe benefit program. Nor does the existence of a retirement plan in a business disqualify it from consideration as a prospect. A 401(k) plan can be added to existing profit-sharing and stock bonus plans. The business doesn't even have to have current or retained profits. A business just starting up and not yet earning a profit may establish a profit-sharing plan with 401(k) provisions.

■ IDENTIFYING SPECIFIC PROSPECTS

Generally, prospects for a 401(k) plan are identified in the same ways as the prospects for other products. Current clients are a basic source of names. If the client is a business owner, then the owner is not only a source of referrals but also a prospect. Other sources include centers of influence, friends and acquaintances, direct mail, business and pension directories, and so on. Sponsoring seminars on 401(k)s is also an effective way to identify prospects.

■ OBTAINING THE INTERVIEW

Once a specific prospect has been identified, the next step is to obtain an interview. Although the prospect may be telephoned with or without any preliminary contact, you may prefer to precede the phone call with a preapproach letter. This is a brief, individually typed letter outlining the products and services available and requesting a meeting at the prospect's convenience. This often "warms up" the prospect, familiarizes him or her with your name and paves the way for an introductory phone call.

Sample Approaches

A sample preapproach letter and telephone conversation are found on the following pages. These are only suggested formats and should be modified to fit your particular requirements.

MAKING A 401(k) PRESENTATION

The prospect you have identified and approached should be someone with the authority to make the initial buying decision. Generally, this person will be the company's chief executive. There is no point in conducting an interview with someone if this person is not in a position to make the decision to buy.

Initial Interview

The interview process will involve at least two different meetings with the prospect. The initial interview has three primary goals: (1) to create enthusiasm in the employer for the 401(k) plan; (2) to obtain basic employee data from which a proposal may be made; and (3) to obtain enough information about the employer's needs and desires to design the proper plan.

Creating the needed enthusiasm on the part of the prospect requires an effective sales presentation, and the most effective presentation generally is one that makes use of

ILL. 7.1 ■ *Sample 401(k) Preapproach Letter*

Dear M__. Prospect:

As a business owner, no one needs to tell you how important it is to attract and retain quality employees. Even so, the cost of fringe benefits often approaches 50 percent of salary.

However, there is a plan available that provides you and your employees with a way to:

- reduce current income taxes by deferring pretax dollars to the plan
- earn tax-deferred interest on the amounts
- receive favorable tax treatment when the funds are withdrawn at retirement

All of this can be provided by a 401(k) plan—a cost-effective, flexible program that can be designed to fit your particular needs.

I'll call in a few days to arrange a meeting at your convenience.

Sincerely,

ILL. 7.2 ■ *Sample 401(k) Preapproach Phone Call*

AGENT: Hello, M__. Prospect, this is ________________________ with ____________________. Are you free to talk for a moment?

PROSPECT: Yes, I have a free minute.

AGENT: Fine. M__. Prospect, as a business owner no one needs to tell you how important it is to attract and retain quality employees. Even so, the cost of fringe benefits often approaches 50 percent of salary. Are fringe benefits a costly part of your business?

PROSPECT: Yes, and the cost is rising every year.

AGENT: You should be familiar with the 401(k) plan, which is a cost-effective method of providing you and your employees with a way to reduce current income taxes by deferring pretax dollars, earn tax-deferred interest and receive favorable tax treatment when funds are withdrawn at retirement. Would you have any objection to my discussing this new plan with you? I want to show you how a 401(k) plan through my company is advantageous to you and your company. I'll be in your area tomorrow morning/afternoon. What time is convenient for you?

PROSPECT: I have a deadline to meet tomorrow. Won't have time to see you. Can you make it next Monday?

AGENT: I can make it first thing Monday morning. Is 8:00 A.M. convenient for you?

PROSPECT: That's fine. By the way, what did you say your name was?

sales visuals. A presentation with visuals is stronger than one without them because the prospect is receiving information through the senses of hearing and sight.

In addition to increasing the impact of the sales presentation with the use of both sight and hearing rather than hearing alone, the visual sales presentation also enjoys other advantages. These are:

- helping to get more complete interviews because the prospect usually will not cut off the interview before the visual presentation is concluded;

- serving as an interview guide by helping you to stay on track despite answering questions and objections;
- making it easier to refer back to points already covered; and
- leaving you free to pay attention to delivery, timing and prospect reactions.

To be effective, the presentation must arouse the prospect's interest in the 401(k) plan to the extent that he or she feels an inescapable need for the product, establish the prospect's confidence in you as the person most able to handle this service and secure the employee data or other information necessary to make a proper study for the prospect. To accomplish these goals, the presentation must be simple, clear and complete. Further, it must appeal to the prospect's enlightened self-interest. The presentation answers the often unspoken question, "What's in it for me?" For a business owner, that question is answered not only by showing how a 401(k) will benefit the owner as an employee but also how it will help the business itself.

An effective visual sales presentation can be an extremely effective sales tool. Visual sales aids are usually available from several different sources, including the insurance company's home office. Or you may choose to develop your own presentation tools.

Techniques for Handling Objections

After, and during, the sales presentation, be prepared to answer questions and counter objections raised by the prospect. A discussion on how to answer all objections is beyond the scope of this manual, but the major point to remember is that objections are often requests for additional information. By voicing concerns, the prospect is providing you with clues to the direction the sales presentation should take. Turn objections into selling points and use them as another step to the sale.

It is often possible to anticipate objections from prospects even before you call on them, if you are familiar with their thinking. This puts you in a favorable position, not only to state the objection in your own words but to have a prepared answer to the objection. For example, when talking to an employer who prefers to deal on a cash-only basis, you might say:

"You may be wondering what would happen if you just gave your employees cash. Let me explain the tax consequences to your employees and to your business."

In addition, anticipating objections impresses your prospects with your appreciation of their problems and your fairness in stating their side of the question first.

Finally, anticipating a prospect's objection brings the issue into the open, enabling you to control the interview. This is particularly important if the prospect hesitates to state the real reason why he or she does not want to buy.

Specific Answers to Objections

There usually is more than one way to answer objections. The following are solid, field-tested answers. The technique used may not be the one you would choose in a given situation, but it serves to demonstrate how techniques can be the basis for specific answers.

Objection #1: "It costs too much."

"You mean that you can't afford it. But with its tax advantages to yourself personally and to your employees, you can't afford not to buy this plan. Let's talk about what 401(k) saves you in tax dollars that will more than pay for this plan."

or . . .

"You say that you can do better with your money? 401(k) funds access favorable investment vehicles and you can choose the investment vehicle in which you want your funds to accumulate. The best part is, if you ever need a loan, you can use the funds in your 401(k) plan. How many other investments permit you to do that? Let me show you the choices available for your funds and those of your employees."

Objection #2: "My employees won't participate" or "My employees won't appreciate it."

"There are very good reasons why implementing a 401(k) plan would encourage employee commitment and loyalty. Many employees will like the opportunity to purchase individual life insurance with pretax income. You, their employer, will be perceived as a caring individual, concerned about helping your employees defer their income taxes, matching a certain percentage of their contributions and offering this option to an employee who is promoted. Part of my job is to present this plan to your employees and show them the advantages."

Objection #3: "A 401(k) plan is too difficult to administer."

"Administration of a 401(k) plan cannot be left in the hands of inexperienced individuals. Not only does my company handle a wide variety of investment options, but it also has a recordkeeping system to handle frequent changes in contributions and transfers among the various options. Our 401(k) department does nothing but administer 401(k)s, leaving you and your staff free to keep your business productive and profitable. Here's what my company can do for you."

After kindling the prospect's enthusiasm for 401(k)s and answering any questions or objections, basic data is needed in order to prepare a proposal to be presented at the next meeting.

ILL. 7.3 ■ *Sample Company Data Sheet*

Name of Company ______________________________

Street ____________________ City ____________________

State ____________________ Phone ____________________

Type of Business ______________________________

☐ Corporation ☐ Partnership ☐ Sole Proprietorship

Predecessor Business (if any) ______________________________

☐ Corporation ☐ Partnership ☐ Sole Proprietorship

Date Present Company Established ______________________________

Fiscal Year Ends ______________________________

Accounting Method ☐ Cash ☐ Accrual

COMPANY OFFICERS

Name	Position	Percentage of Stock, Partnership or Sole Proprietorship
____________	____________	____________
____________	____________	____________
____________	____________	____________

OTHER BENEFIT PROGRAMS

Pension Plan ______________________________

Profit-Sharing Plan ______________________________

Bonus Plan ______________________________

Group Insurance Plan ______________________________

ILL. 7.4 ■ *Reverse of Sample Company Data Sheet*

GENERAL REMARKS

EMPLOYEE INFORMATION

After how many years of employment does employee turnover subside? ______________________

Number of hours in basic work week? ______________________

Is employee turnover higher under a minimum age (i.e., age 20–age 25)? ______________________

If possible, does employer desire a specific group of people to be covered by plan? If so, check on census sheet. ______________________

OTHER REMARKS

____

____

____

____

____

____

____

____

____

____

____

____

____

____

____

____

____

____

ILL. 7.5 ■ *Sample Employee Census*

NAME OR CODE	SEX	DATE OF BIRTH	EMPLOYMENT DATE	BASIC COMPENSATION	PER WK./ MO.	JOB TITLE

Essential data needed to prepare a realistic proposal tailored to the employer's unique situation include the following:

- the prospect's prime reason for wanting a 401(k) plan;
- the particular group or employees that the prospect would like the plan to benefit;
- a complete census of the company's employees;
- information on existing employee benefit plans; and
- the identity of the firm's accountant and attorney.

This is certainly not a complete list, but it does provide an idea of the scope of the information needed. Illustrations 7.3, 7.4 and 7.5 show typical data sheets requesting information required to prepare a realistic proposal.

The interview should be closed—after first obtaining a date for the next meeting—by providing the prospect with a brief overview of the remaining steps in establishing a 401(k) plan.

The Second Interview

The purpose of this second meeting with the prospect is to present the proposal and close the sale. However, this view of a successful 401(k) sale requiring only two interviews to obtain a close is often optimistic. The process may involve a number of meetings over weeks or months as changes are made in the proposal and details worked out.

Of course, not every proposal presentation is going to lead to a successful close. However, a successful close is more likely if you are sensitive to timing in the sales process and follow some standard closing rules. As to timing, sales are often lost when the employer is pushed too soon for a commitment or a presentation is continued after the employer has already committed. Successful closes depend on being able to understand what the prospect is saying, with both words and body language.

Standard closing rules to keep in mind include the following:

- Don't ask "yes" or "no" questions because these questions stop the flow in the sales process and leave little room for "side-stepping" a negative response.
- Use implied consent by assuming that silence means a favorable response.
- Ask for small decisions that add up to a commitment.

- Restate the benefits, which often are forgotten in the closing process.
- Proceed after answering objections rather than becoming side-tracked.
- Don't make the prospect angry if the sale is lost. Leave room for the prospect to change the decision later.

SUMMARY

Identifying employers and companies interested in a 401(k) plan may at first seem daunting. However, 401(k) prospects may be uncovered with the same methods used to identify prospects for other products. Once a potential client is identified, obtaining an initial interview is the next step. The initial interview is used to generate interest in a 401(k) plan and obtain basic information to prepare a proposal. A proposed plan should not be presented until a second or subsequent interview. Follow-up meetings should be used to answer any questions or objections raised by the prospect.

CHAPTER 7 QUESTIONS FOR REVIEW

1. In the initial interview, which of the following is NOT a primary goal?

   A. To create enthusiasm in the employer for the 401(k) plan
   B. To obtain basic employee data
   C. To obtain information about the employer's needs
   D. To present a 401(k) proposal

2. Which of the following is a possible response to an employer's objection that a 401(k) plan is too difficult to administer?

   A. "Plan administration is very simple and can be done by your secretary."
   B. "I am not prepared to answer your question right now but I will get back to you."
   C. "The IRS is very lenient about plan administration, so it is an area that does not merit our time or attention."
   D. "My company is very experienced at administrating 401(k) plans and has an excellent track record. This leaves you free to keep your business productive and profitable."

3. Which of the following data is NOT needed to prepare a 401(k) proposal?

   A. The names and the number of dependents for each employee
   B. The prospect's prime reason for wanting a 401(k) plan
   C. Information on existing employee benefit plans
   D. The complete census of the company's employees

4. The purpose of the second interview is to

   A. meet the prospect and generate enthusiasm for a 401(k) plan
   B. present a 401(k) proposal and attempt to close the sale
   C. tour company facilities
   D. meet with company employees interested in a 401(k) plan

5. Which of the following would NOT be considered a standard closing rule?

   A. Ask for small decisions that add up to a commitment.
   B. Restate the benefits of the proposal presented.
   C. Proceed after answering objections rather than becoming side-tracked.
   D. Ask "yes" or "no" questions as much as possible.

8

Plan Installation

Plan installation is not done by a single individual but by a team of experts. Although you will not be directly involved in this highly technical final step, as the liaison between the team of experts and your client, an understanding of the basics of plan administration is critical. The purpose of this chapter is to describe how plans are written, reporting and disclosure requirements that are necessary to maintain their tax-favored status and the use of fiduciaries. It is imperative that you possess this background knowledge of installation and administration of 401(k) plans to enhance your understanding of procedures so that you may speak confidently and knowledgeably with your client.

The purpose of this chapter is to provide a brief overview of the process of installation and administration of a 401(k) plan. Your role is far from over once the employer has been convinced of the benefits of a 401(k) plan and the sale has been closed. The installation of the plan can require the cooperation of many parties: the employer, the attorney, the accountant and the trustee, if any. As the creator of the plan proposal, you are a key figure with an active role in orchestrating and coordinating the efforts of the other professionals. Your continuing service to the plan is not only important to smooth plan installation but also is essential to retaining the employer as a client in the competitive qualified plan business.

WRITING THE PLAN

The execution of a written instrument is the first formal step that brings a 401(k) plan into existence. The plan must be spelled out in a plan document; this is one of the general requirements of a qualified plan. Although you should be familiar with the plan's content, preparation of the document is the sole responsibility of the employer's attorney. However, your home office or firm usually can be of considerable help to the attorney. Most organizations interested in attracting 401(k) plan business have created sample plans. These sample plans are normally made available to lawyers who are interested in drafting an instrument that will provide for the benefits and funding vehicles outlined in the 401(k) proposal. It is the lawyer's responsibility to see that these sample plans fit the employer's situation.

To simplify the procedure in filing a qualified plan for approval, the Internal Revenue Service introduced master and prototype plans. Under this approach, the sponsoring organization, such as an insurance company, bank or mutual fund, files with the IRS a replica of the plan it intends to sell. Once such a plan is approved by the IRS, then an insurance company, for example, is in a position to offer its particular plan for use by an employer. If a company wishes to adopt a particular master or prototype plan as its own, it must accept the plan as it stands. Based on the advice of its attorney, the employer merely fills in the blanks found in the instrument and executes it. Of course, the employer may have its counsel draft a plan from scratch if the employer does not wish to use a master or prototype plan.

Although master and prototype plans are similar, there is a distinction between the two types. Master plans are preapproved by the IRS. However, any changes in the number or eligibility of employees require that the plan be reviewed to ensure that it continues to be qualified. Master plans require that the service provider insurance company provide administrative and investment management services. Master plans will be updated by the insurance company to meet changes in the law.

Prototype plans are not preapproved and as such usually are used only as samples. However, a prototype plan can be submitted to the IRS for approval and become a qualified plan. The plan sponsor has the responsibility to update the document to meet changes in the law.

It is important to keep in mind the effect of IRS approval of a master or prototype plan or trust. Approval means that the IRS considers the plan or trust acceptable from the standpoint of formal compliance with the applicable tax code provisions. This approval does not mean that the use of a master or prototype arrangement by an employer will automatically qualify that employer's particular plan.

Trusteed Plans

401(k) plans established by small and medium-sized businesses often are administered under a trust agreement. In such cases, an employer enters into a trust agreement with the appointed trustees. Employers may appoint as many trustees as desired; however, only trustees who are capable of assuming the fiduciary responsibilities that go along with the job should be considered. (These responsibilities will be briefly covered later in the chapter.) It is through the trust agreement that the employer delegates to the trustees the investment power and control over the plan. When a plan is financed through a trust instrument, it is normally the responsibility of the trustees to administer the plan, in addition to investing the funds. It is always the duty of the trustees to see that the provisions of the trust are properly carried out.

Board of Directors' Approval

For a corporation, the board of directors must adopt a resolution approving the plan. Formal authorization for the plan and the investment in it must come from the board. Usually, if the officers of the company are thoroughly sold on the advantages of the plan, approval by the board of directors follows as a matter of course. Therefore, it is customary for the company's attorney to prepare the necessary forms in advance of the board meeting, including the board resolution adopting the plan and the formal trust instrument. Then, on obtaining board approval, the proper members of the board can immediately sign the resolution and execute the trust agreement. Once the plan is accepted by the board, the instrument then may be presented to the administrators or trustees in order to set the plan in motion.

Initial Contribution

In addition to the execution of a written instrument, a contribution must be made to bring the plan into being. If a plan is administered by a trustee or custodian, contributions must be made to such an administrator who, in turn, maintains the records called for by the plan.

■ PRESENTATION AND ENROLLMENT

The next step in installing a 401(k) plan is to make the written announcement to the employees. This is required for tax qualification and regulatory purposes. Usually this announcement is accomplished by means of a letter prepared over the signature of the president of the company and sent to all employees advising them of the action of the board of directors in adopting the plan for their benefit.

The initial announcement highlights the plan and names the responsible parties. A plan description booklet, describing the plan in detail, also may be included. Also accompanying the announcement and description of the plan are the necessary forms for the employee to complete in order to become a plan participant.

Because a high rate of participation is necessary to a successful 401(k), the enrollment process should be carefully mapped out, and the letter to the employees should not be the only effort to communicate the plan's details. The basics of what the 401(k) is and the benefits of participation can be conveyed to employees through brochures, newsletters, pay envelope inserts, in-house magazines and a number of other ways.

After the word has been spread through these methods, one or more group meetings should be conducted, depending on the number of employees, to explain the 401(k). A tape/slide show or flip chart presentation might be used. Although it is important for the employer to convey its support for the 401(k) in the group meeting, in some cases the presence of an employer representative at the meeting can inhibit the tough questions that employees might otherwise ask about the plan. One solution might be for the employer representative to explain the purpose of the meeting, reaffirm the employer's support for the 401(k), introduce the plan representative and then discreetly leave.

Finally, the group meeting should be followed up by private meetings with the employees over the next few days or weeks. This private meeting can serve to reinforce points already made about the 401(k), answer questions and overcome objections. Also, this meeting provides the opportunity to complete the necessary forms for participation, including life insurance applications.

Applications for Insurance

If a participant elects to buy insurance or an annuity under the plan, the employee signs the insurance application as the annuitant or insured, as the case may be. The trustee signs the application as the applicant. The application usually is worded so that all of the incidents of ownership, except the right to change the beneficiary, are vested in the trustee, subject to the terms of the plan agreement. A medical exam is required in individual policy plans where guaranteed issue underwriting is not available.

■ ADVANCE DETERMINATION

Because the favorable tax advantages of 401(k)s depend solely on compliance with the applicable statutes and regulations, it is helpful to know when going into the plan whether or not it qualifies. Remember that even use of an approved master or prototype plan does not guarantee that an employer's particular plan will pass muster.

To aid the parties involved in determining if a retirement plan does qualify, the IRS will issue a letter of determination or private letter ruling upon request. The letter may be issued either in advance of the plan's installation or after it has been established. Although a letter of determination is not required, the technical requirements of a 401(k) are sufficiently involved to make such a letter highly important. The employer's attorney usually handles the necessary procedure to qualify the plan, but you can be helpful in assembling necessary data. Even though the letter may be issued in advance of installation, the general practice is to first establish the plan and then proceed with details of its approval. Generally, to gain approval any necessary modifications to an existing plan can be made easily. Advance-of-installation approval usually is reserved for those situations where the plan has some questionable features.

SUMMARY

Plan installation is a highly technical process and is the final step prior to implementation of a 401(k) plan. During plan installation the plan is written, approved by the company board of directors and an initial plan contribution is made. The plan is then communicated to employees and the enrollment process begins. The agent or planning professional who created the original 401(k) plan proposal is a key figure during plan installation and plays an active role in orchestrating and coordinating the efforts of other professionals.

CHAPTER 8 QUESTIONS FOR REVIEW

1. What is the difference between a master plan and a prototype plan?

   A. A master plan receives preapproval from the IRS but a prototype plan does not.
   B. A prototype plan receives preapproval from the IRS but a master plan does not.
   C. A master plan is written on company stationery but a prototype plan is not.
   D. A prototype plan is written on company stationery but a master plan is not.

2. When a plan is financed through a trust instrument, who of the following is normally responsible for plan administration?

   A. Lawyer
   B. Trustee
   C. Accountant
   D. Employer

3. Formal authorization for a 401(k) plan and investment in the plan must come from

   A. the lawyer
   B. human resources
   C. the company president
   D. the board of directors

4. In order for a 401(k) plan to be qualified for tax and regulatory purposes, a written announcement must be made to the

   A. board of directors
   B. employees
   C. company creditors
   D. plan trustee

5. To ensure that a 401(k) plan is in compliance with applicable statutes and regulations, most plan sponsors request from the IRS a

   A. certificate of good standing
   B. determination hearing
   C. letter of determination or private letter ruling
   D. compliance notice

9

Plan Administration

The administration of a 401(k) plan is the responsibility of the plan administrator. Because the plan administrator is responsible for the security of the plan's assets—both the investment and management of the assets—and for the proper handling of plan benefits, he or she is also a plan fiduciary. A breach of fiduciary duties with respect to the plan may result in liability to the plan or to plan participants and beneficiaries. In addition, civil penalties may be imposed for breaches of fiduciary duty and excise taxes are imposed on prohibited transactions. This chapter will provide an overview of the basics of plan administration requirements.

PLAN ADMINISTRATION IN GENERAL

Administration of a 401(k) plan may be handled in one of several ways:

- by the employer;
- by the insurance company or other organization providing the funding products; or
- by a third-party administrator (TPA).

A 401(k) plan is somewhat more expensive to maintain than other defined contribution plans. The fact that they offer employees several investment options means that they require more careful tracking of accounts by the plan's administrator. Also, the matching employee funds feature in many plans creates an additional administrative burden. The extra administration required because of the flexibility and options offered by a 401(k) makes it worthwhile for the employer to hire a plan administrator. Insurance companies and other plan administrators provide those services through their 401(k) administration departments with the purchase of their 401(k) funding products.

Annual Servicing

A 401(k) plan will not continue to function for long unless it receives regular professional administration. Even if the federal government did not require it, employers should be concerned about the proper ongoing administration of their retirement plans. After all, the client almost always has a personal interest in the ultimate financial security provided by the plan.

Each anniversary of the plan is generally the time to review the plan and take any major administrative steps required to see that it operates properly. This usually involves plan-year-end analysis and accounting, analysis of the current or prospective year and making certain contributions. Contributions from employee salary reductions and employer matching funds are made periodically during the plan year.

The annual review also provides an opportunity to contact participants about the purchase of life insurance products as an investment option. The agent or planning professional can review the situation of employees who already have insurance with the purpose of readjusting the level of insurance to meet the employee's current needs; he or she also has the chance to convince participants who do not own insurance through the 401(k) of the value of the products. Finally, the annual review is an excellent time to approach nonparticipants about the benefits of the 401(k) plan and the insurance products.

■ REPORTING AND DISCLOSURE REQUIREMENTS

In an effort to police qualified retirement plans more closely, ERISA mandated that the persons responsible for administering the plan must file certain reports with government agencies and disclose certain information to plan participants and beneficiaries. Some reports must be filed with the Department of Labor, others with the Department of the Treasury. The following is a brief overview of the filing and disclosure requirements for a typical 401(k) plan.

Filings with the Secretary of Labor

Generally, the following documents must be filed with the Secretary of Labor:

1. *Plan description.* The plan administrator must file a plan description, usually within 120 days after the plan is established.

2. *Updated plan description.* An updated plan description must be filed at least every five years after the filing of the initial plan description.

3. *Summary plan description.* As explained later, plan participants and beneficiaries must be furnished with a summary plan description. A copy of this also must be filed with the Secretary of Labor within 120 days after the plan is established. The document must be written in a manner designed to be understood by the average plan participant and must be accurate and precise enough to reasonably inform the participants and beneficiaries of their rights and obligations under the plan.

4. *Plan modifications and changes in plan description information.* Under the strict terms of ERISA, if there is any material modification in plan terms or any change in plan information, the administrator must file a statement of that change with the Department of Labor 60 days after the change occurs or is adopted. However, plan administrators are now required only to file a summary description of plan changes within 210 days after the end of the plan year in which the change is adopted. This means, rather than the 60-day statutory deadline, only the 210-day deadline need be met for filing plan changes. The 210-day deadline also applies to the disclosure of plan changes to participants and beneficiaries.

5. *Annual report.* The administrator must file an annual report with the Secretary of Labor. The report generally is due within 210 days after the close of the plan year.

Filings with the Secretary of the Treasury (IRS)

The following information must be filed with the Treasury Department:

1. *Annual registration statement.* The 5500 series of forms must be filed by the last day of the seventh month after the plan year ends.

2. *Notification of change in status.* The plan administrator must notify the IRS of any changes in the name of the plan or in the name or address of the plan administrator or of the termination of the plan or its merger or consolidation with any other plan.

3. *Annual information return.* Annual information returns are filed by the employer or plan administrator with information relating to the qualifications, financial condition and operation of the plan.

4. *Information returns for distribution to participants.*

5. *Miscellaneous returns.*

Disclosures to Plan Participants and Beneficiaries

The following information must be published and furnished to plan participants and their beneficiaries:

1. *Summary plan description.* This is the same summary plan description that the administrator is required to file with the Secretary of Labor. It must be furnished to plan participants and beneficiaries within the later of 120 days after the plan is established or 90 days after the individual becomes a participant or starts receiving benefits as a beneficiary.

2. *Updated summary plan description.* This is the same as the form that must be filed with the Secretary of Labor every five years.

3. *Summary annual report.* Within 210 days after the close of the fiscal year of the plan, the plan administrator must furnish each participant and beneficiary with a copy of the statements and schedules completed for the annual report.

4. *Summary description of plan modifications and information changes.* This information must be furnished within 210 days after the close of the plan year. If the modification is incorporated in the summary plan description, no separate summary of the modification need be provided.

5. *Annual registration statement.* A plan administrator must furnish a statement of rights to any participant who, during the plan year, separated from service covered by the plan, is entitled to a deferred vested benefit under the plan as of the end of the plan year, and to whom retirement benefits were not paid under the plan during that plan year.

6. *Statement to terminating employees.* When a plan participant terminates employment, the participant must be furnished information relating to the taxable status of various distributions.

7. *Plan participant's request.* Upon written request, the plan administrator must furnish to the participant a copy of the latest updated summary plan description, plan description and various other reports and agreements relating to the plan.

8. *Joint and survivor annuity explanation.* If a plan participant under the plan has an election as to a joint and survivor annuity, the administrator must furnish the participant with an explanation of the option.

9. *Employee benefit statements.* Upon written request, the administrator must furnish to any plan participant or beneficiary a statement of total and nonforfeitable benefits under the plan.

10. *Claim procedures.* Every employee benefit plan must provide adequate notice in writing to any participant or beneficiary whose claim for a benefit

ILL. 9.1 ■ *Communication Vehicles*

A wide variety of vehicles are available to plan sponsors to communicate plan information. The traditional "hard copy" method for disseminating plan information to participants continues to prevail. However, videos, computer hardware and software, as well as direct personal contact, are used by a significant number of plan sponsors.

Written Materials

Handbooks	53%
Employee newsletter	61%
Pamphlets	60%
Newsletter/magazine devoted to 401(k) plan investment and savings	48%
SPD	73%
Computer-generated investment history/earnings	27%
Computer-generated comprehensive benefit statements	35%
Other	6%

Note: Respondents were permitted to select more than one item.

Source: BUCK CONSULTANTS

under the plan has been denied. The notice must give the reasons for the denial, and an opportunity for a review must be provided.

11. *Statement of rights and obligations.* The administrator must furnish each participant and beneficiary with a statement of his or her rights and obligations under the plan.

■ FIDUCIARIES

A person acts in a fiduciary capacity when the business he or she transacts involves money or property held for the benefit of others when there is a relationship implying or necessitating confidence, trust and good faith on their part. Under ERISA, a person is a fiduciary with respect to a qualified plan to the extent he or she exercises any discretionary control or authority over management of the plan or disposition of its assets. The definition of fiduciary includes a person who gives investment advice for a fee or other compensation, direct or indirect, or who has authority or responsibility for plan administration. Each plan must specify a named fiduciary, but this may not relieve others from being fiduciaries.

A fiduciary is considered a disqualified person, which means that such a person may not enter into specified prohibited transactions. In addition to fiduciaries, disqualified persons include, among others, persons providing services to the plan, 50 percent or greater owners of the business and employers with employees covered by the plan. Nearly every person or business connected with administering the plan fits into one of the several categories of disqualified persons. For example, a life insurance agent probably would qualify as a fiduciary, except for the exemption discussed later, because he or she handles funds of others whose interests are to be protected.

A fiduciary may not become involved in any transaction (a prohibited transaction) where another disqualified person (a party-in-interest) is also party to the transaction. For example, prohibited transactions prevent a fiduciary from furnishing goods, services or facilities to a party-in-interest or selling, exchanging or leasing property held in the plan to a party-in-interest.

The Department of Labor has issued a number of prohibited transaction exemptions (PTEs), and one of these, PTE 77-9, directly applies to the transactions normally conducted involving insurance agents or brokers, pension consultants, insurance companies and investment company principal underwriters who might be considered fiduciaries because of their activities relating to the plan. An exemption is granted for a transaction that involves, among others: (1) receipt, directly or indirectly, of commissions from an insurance company by an insurance agent or broker or a pension consultant in connection with the purchase with plan assets of an insurance or annuity product; and (2) purchase (and premium payment) to an insurance company that is a service provider.

The exemption is granted if: (1) the transaction is carried out in the normal course of business; (2) the transaction is on terms no less favorable to the plan than the plan could get from an outside party; and (3) the total compensation received by the agent, broker or pension consultant is reasonable.

To take advantage of the exemption, the agent must: (1) disclose to the fiduciary the amount to be received in commissions, expressed as a percentage of gross annual payments for the first year and each succeeding renewal year, to be paid to the agent; and (2) disclose any relationship that exists between the agent and the company whose products are being recommended.

■ SUMMARY

Plan administration is an ongoing process involving not only a formal annual plan review but also reporting and disclosure standards—both for employees and the IRS—that require monitoring. For most employers, extensive plan administration requirements make it worthwhile to hire a professional plan administrator. Because the plan administrator is responsible for the security of plan assets and for the proper handling of plan benefits, he or she is also a plan fiduciary.

CHAPTER 9 QUESTIONS FOR REVIEW

1. Administration of a 401(k) plan may be handled by any of the following EXCEPT

   A. the employer
   B. the insurance company or other organization providing the funding products
   C. a third-party administrator
   D. beneficiaries of employees

2. A 401(k) plan must be reviewed

   A. annually
   B. quarterly
   C. every six months
   D. every three years

3. A plan description must be filed within 120 days after the plan is established with the

   A. Secretary of the Treasury (the IRS)
   B. Secretary of Labor
   C. Secretary of Defense
   D. Secretary of State

4. Plan participants must be furnished with all of the following EXCEPT

   A. a summary plan description
   B. a summary annual report
   C. the names of all plan beneficiaries
   D. an employee benefit statement

5. Under which of the following acts is a person a fiduciary with respect to a qualified plan to the extent he or she exercises any discretionary control or authority over management of the plan or disposition of its assets?

   A. COBRA
   B. TRA '86
   C. ERISA
   D. OBRA

10

SIMPLE Plans

In order to encourage small businesses to provide expanded retirement coverage, Congress enacted the Small Business Job Protection Act. This act created a type of retirement plan called a Savings Incentive Match Plan for Employees (SIMPLE plan), which certain employers may adopt. According to the act, an employer can structure a SIMPLE plan as either an IRA or 401(k) qualified cash or deferred arrangement (CODA). Because SIMPLE plans are not subject to all the rules applicable to qualified plans, small employers may be interested in establishing a SIMPLE plan in lieu of another qualified retirement plan. This chapter gives an overview of how SIMPLE plans work and explains the rules applicable to such plans.

According to the Employee Benefit Research Institute, only about 19 percent of workers in firms with less than 20 employees are covered by a retirement plan, and only about 15 percent actually participate. Responding to the need to encourage small business to provide retirement benefits for employees, Congress created SIMPLE plans. As part of the inducement to attract employers to adopt such plans, many of the complex rules applicable to qualified plans, such as the top-heavy rules and nondiscrimination tests, have been eliminated. This chapter describes the type of employers that may adopt SIMPLE plans as well as how these plans work.

WHAT IS A SIMPLE PLAN?

A SIMPLE plan is a type of retirement plan that can take the form of either an IRA, called a SIMPLE IRA, or a cash or deferred arrangement plan, called a SIMPLE 401(k) plan. With both types of SIMPLE plans, an employee makes a contribution, within set limits, to his or her individual account through salary reduction and the employer transfers this amount to the employee's account. The employer in turn is required to make an annual contribution to each participating employee's account, as discussed below in more detail. The contributions are then deposited into a trust account for the employee and grow tax-free until distributed. As with 401(k) plans, an employer who has adopted a SIMPLE plan provides employees with a way to:

- decrease taxable income
- establish a savings/retirement plan
- allow retirement savings to grow on a tax-deferred basis
- tailor the fund to their own investment goals

CREATING A SIMPLE PLAN

Although SIMPLE plans are intended to be a retirement savings vehicle for small businesses, not all small employers can adopt such plans. Instead, only those employers that meet the specific eligibility requirements discussed below may establish a SIMPLE plan.

Eligible Employers

First, only employers with no more than 100 employees may adopt a SIMPLE plan. However, the term "employer" includes *related employers,* such as trades or businesses under common control (whether incorporated or not), controlled groups of corporations, and affiliated service groups. As a result, a business employing 80 eligible employees cannot establish a SIMPLE plan if it has a subsidiary with more than 20 eligible employees.

In addition, an employer may not create a SIMPLE plan if it already maintains another qualified plan. A "qualified plan" includes a qualified retirement plan, a qualified annuity plan, a governmental plan, a tax-sheltered annuity or a simplified employee pension. An employer will be treated as having another plan if it or a predecessor employer maintained a qualified plan and contributions were made, or benefits accrued, during the period beginning with the year the SIMPLE plan became effective and ending with the year for which the determination is being made.

Two-Year Grace Period

Often, an employer may initially employ fewer than 100 employees but may exceed this number over time. In this case, can the employer continue to maintain a SIMPLE plan? If an employer with a SIMPLE plan no longer meets the eligibility requirements, the employer may continue to maintain the SIMPLE plan for two years after the last year in which it was eligible. At the end of this two-year grace period, however, the employer must discontinue the SIMPLE plan.

Participation Requirements

An employer must open its SIMPLE plan to every employee who:

1. received at least $5,000 in compensation from the employer during any two preceding years; and

2. is reasonably expected to receive at least $5,000 in compensation during the current year.

Keep in mind, however, that an employee must have earned only $5,000 in *any* two preceding years and not necessarily in the *immediately* preceding two years. In addition, unlike 401(k) plans, SIMPLE plans are not subject to the rule requiring 40 percent of all eligible employees to participate in the plan. As a result, an employer can establish a SIMPLE plan even if only one or two of its employees wants to participate.

The Small Business Act also permits self-employed individuals to participate in a SIMPLE plan. However, an employer may exclude its nonresident alien employees and employees covered under a collective bargaining agreement from participating in the plan.

Election to Participate in a SIMPLE Plan

Each eligible employee can elect to participate in a SIMPLE plan during the 60-day period before the beginning of the year (or during the 60-day period before the employee becomes eligible to participate). During this period, an employee may also change how much he or she has previously elected to contribute to the SIMPLE account. According to the Small Business Act, a plan can also permit (but is not required to permit) participants to modify the amount they are contributing to their account at any time during the year.

If an employee no longer wishes to participate in a SIMPLE plan, he or she may terminate participation at any time during the year by simply discontinuing contributions. However, a plan can provide that if an employee terminates participation, that employee may not resume participation until the following year.

CONTRIBUTIONS

Employee contributions to a SIMPLE plan come from deferred income. However, there are restrictions that limit the amount a plan participant can defer as well as rules that mandate the amount an employer must contribute to an employee's SIMPLE account.

Employee Contribution Limits

According to the Small Business Act, an employee may contribute up to $6,000 each year to his or her SIMPLE account. The $6,000 limit is indexed for inflation in $500 increments. In addition, an employee's deferrals must be expressed as a percentage of compensation rather than as a flat dollar amount. Employers must contribute an employee's elective deferrals to his or her plan account no later than 30 days after the last day of the month for which the deferrals are made.

Employer Matching Contributions

Employers must make annual contributions to their employees' SIMPLE accounts pursuant to one of the following formulas.

Matching Contribution Formula. An employer may match contributions made by an employee on a dollar-for-dollar basis, up to 3 percent of that employee's compensation for the year. However, an employer may contribute as little as 1 percent of each employee's compensation for a given year. In order to use a reduced matching percentage, an employer must notify employees of this decision within a reasonable time before the 60-day election period during which employees decide whether to participate in the SIMPLE plan. However, an employer cannot elect a lower percentage for more than two out of any five years. It is important to note that employers with SIMPLE plans structured as 401(k) plans do not have the option of reducing their matching contributions to less than 3 percent of an employee's compensation.

Two Percent Nonelective Contribution. Alternatively, an employer may make a nonelective contribution of 2 percent of compensation for each eligible employee. If the employer uses this formula, it must notify each eligible employee of its choice within a reasonable period of time before the period when an employee decides whether to participate in the SIMPLE plan.

No matter which contribution formula an employer selects, the employer must make matching contributions to each employee's account no later than the date its tax return for that tax year is due, including any extensions. Finally, no contributions other than employee elective contributions and required employer matching contributions (or, alternatively, required employer nonelective contributions) can be made to a SIMPLE account.

Nondiscrimination Rules

When a SIMPLE 401(k) plan complies with the above contribution rules, the plan is deemed to have satisfied the nondiscrimination rules applicable to 401(k) plans. Thus, SIMPLE 401(k) plans will not be subject to the 401(k) top-heavy rules or nondiscrimination tests. However, the other qualified plan rules still apply to such plans.

Vesting

The SIMPLE plan rules require employee elective deferrals to be 100 percent vested at all times. With regard to employer matching contributions, all contributions must vest immediately as well. Thus, an employee's rights in the amounts he or she has deferred to the SIMPLE plan and the amounts contributed by the employer may not be forfeited.

Tax Treatment of Contributions

SIMPLE plans provide a tax incentive for employers: employer contributions to employees' SIMPLE accounts are deductible for the year such contributions were made. However, in order to be able to take a deduction, an employer must make matching contributions by the date its tax return is due, including any extensions. An employer can also deduct amounts it contributed on behalf of an employee under that employee's election.

As with 401(k) plans, employee contributions to a SIMPLE account are excludable from the employee's income for income tax purposes. However, the amount deferred by an employee is subject to Social Security (FICA) and federal unemployment (FUTA) taxes as part of an employee's "wages." Employer matching or nonelective contributions to an employee's SIMPLE account are not viewed as wages and are therefore not subject to either FICA or FUTA taxes.

■ DISTRIBUTIONS

Although the Code is not yet clear regarding how distributions will be taxed, some guidance indicates that distributions from a SIMPLE 401(k) plan will be treated like distributions from a 401(k) plan. See Chapter 4 for a discussion of the specific rules regarding distributions.

REPORTING REQUIREMENTS

In order to ensure that the employer and plan trustee remain accountable to the participants, these parties must disclose certain information to the Secretary of the Treasury, plan participants and beneficiaries on an annual basis. However, neither the plan trustee nor the employer maintaining the SIMPLE plan is required to meet the general reporting requirements of ERISA. The following gives a brief overview of the disclosure requirements for a typical SIMPLE plan.

Trustee Responsibilities

Each year, the trustee of a SIMPLE plan must provide the employer with a summary description containing the following information:

- name and address of the employer and trustee;
- eligibility requirements for participating in the plan;
- plan benefits;
- time and procedure for making salary reduction elections; and
- procedures for, and effect of, making withdrawals (including rollovers) from the plan account.

The trustee must also give each employee participating in the SIMPLE plan an account statement within 30 days after the end of each calendar year. This statement must show the account balance as well as the account activity during the year. In addition, the trustee is required to file an annual report with the Secretary of the Treasury. If the trustee fails to provide the summary description, account statement, or the annual report, a $50 per day penalty will be assessed until such failure is corrected. However, a trustee will not be penalized if the reporting failure was due to reasonable cause.

Employer Responsibilities

Employers maintaining SIMPLE plans must notify employees about their right to make salary reduction contributions under the plan and must describe which contribution alternative the employer has selected. The employer's notice must also include a copy of the summary description prepared by the trustee. Each employee must receive a copy of the notice immediately before the period during which the employee elects whether to participate in the plan. Employers who fail to provide this notice are subject to a $50 per day penalty until notice is given. However, an employer will not be penalized if its failure was due to reasonable cause.

ILL. 10.1 ■ *Advantages of SIMPLE Plans*

Because a SIMPLE plan is designed to accommodate both employees and small businesses, each party will benefit from the creation of such a plan. Like 401(k) plans, SIMPLE plans offer many of the same tax advantages to employees and employers alike. Some of the most significant advantages include the benefits listed below.

Employee Advantages

As with 401(k) plans, the advantages of a SIMPLE plan to the employee center around the favorable income tax treatment in saving money for future retirement.

Reduce Current Income Taxes. Although the amount an employee elects to defer to a SIMPLE account is subject to Social Security taxes, it does not show up on the employee's W-2 form as part of gross income. Because the SIMPLE plan contribution is excluded from gross income, plan participants can realize significant income tax savings by making annual contributions to their account.

Increase Annual Savings. Because plan participants make *pretax* contributions to their accounts, they are able to save more each year. For example, an individual who puts $6,000 in a SIMPLE account deposits the entire amount tax free. On the other hand, if that same individual deposits $6,000 into a savings account for retirement, such contribution must be made with after-tax dollars.

A plan participant also realizes an increase in annual savings because of employer matching contributions. As discussed in Chapter 10, employers must make contributions to each participating employee's account based on one of two contribution formulas. Thus, an employee receives additional retirement money by participating in a SIMPLE plan.

Earnings Are Sheltered from Taxes. Earnings on amounts contributed to a SIMPLE account grow on a tax-deferred basis. A participant does not pay income taxes on earnings or contributions until they are distributed from the SIMPLE plan, generally at retirement. Presumably, when a participant withdraws the funds at retirement, he or she will be in a lower tax bracket and will therefore pay less income tax on the amounts received from the SIMPLE plan.

Automatic Saving. In a typical SIMPLE plan, amounts that employees contribute are automatically deducted from their salaries each pay period. This arrangement provides participants with an easy way to set aside money for retirement and ensures that a certain amount will be saved each month.

Immediate Vesting of Contributions. Unlike 401(k) plans, all contributions made to an employee's account vest immediately, including employer contributions. An employee's right to employer contributions is not dependent upon years of service because such plans are not subject to the vesting schedules applicable to 401(k) plans.

Employer Advantages

Like 401(k) plans, advantages to an employer fall into two categories: those that apply to the employer as an employee and those that apply to the business.

Ability to Participate in SIMPLE Plan. Because a business owner is considered an employee for purposes of SIMPLE plans, the owner enjoys all of the advantages discussed above, including pretax funding of the plan and tax-deferred earnings.

Continued

ILL. 10.1 ■ *Advantages of SIMPLE Plans (Continued)*

Deductible Contributions. Employers with a SIMPLE plan can take a current deduction for their contributions to an employee's account as well as for the contributions made by an employee.

Way to Recruit/Retain Employees. Because few small business enterprises offer retirement plans, establishing a SIMPLE plan might give a business an edge over its competitors in the struggle to retain and recruit employees. Workers may be more likely to want to work for a business that provides a retirement plan than for one that does not.

Administrative Simplicity. A SIMPLE 401(k) plan is deemed to have satisfied the nondiscrimination rules applicable to 401(k) plans if it complies with the following contribution rules: (1) each employee's elective deferrals for the year do not exceed $6,000; (2) the employer either makes a matching contribution of up to 3 percent of the employee's compensation or a 2 percent nonelective contribution of compensation for each eligible employee; and (3) no other contributions are made to the SIMPLE plan. An employer that meets these requirements will also be exempt from the top-heavy plan requirements. Accordingly, it will be easier to administer a SIMPLE plan because the complex nondiscrimination and top-heavy rules are inapplicable to such plans.

In addition, trustees and employers are not required to meet the general reporting requirements imposed by ERISA. Instead, a trustee only has three main reporting requirements. First, it must provide an employer with a summary description of the plan specifications. In addition, it must file a report each year with the Secretary of the Treasury and must provide an account statement to each plan participant. Employers must simply notify employees about their right to participate in the SIMPLE plan and must send them a copy of the summary description prepared by the trustee. Because there are fewer reporting requirements, SIMPLE plans will offer reduced administration costs to small businesses.

Fiduciary Liability

According to the Small Business Act, employers and other plan fiduciaries will not be subject to fiduciary liability when the employee (or beneficiary) is deemed to exercise control over the assets in his or her SIMPLE account. An employee will be treated as exercising control over the account assets upon the earlier of:

1. an affirmative election regarding the initial investment of any contributions;
2. a rollover contribution to another SIMPLE plan account or IRA; or
3. one year after the SIMPLE account is established.

Once an employee (or beneficiary) is treated as exercising control over a SIMPLE plan account, the employer's and trustee's relief from fiduciary liability relates back to the date the account was established. Thus, neither the trustee nor the employer will be held responsible for imprudent investment decisions made by an employee.

SUMMARY

As noted in this chapter, Congress created SIMPLE plans to encourage small businesses to provide retirement benefits for employees. Because SIMPLE plans are not subject to all of the rules that apply to qualified plans, the small employer may be interested in establishing a SIMPLE plan rather than another qualified plan. SIMPLE plans are an excellent choice for small employers seeking an administratively convenient salary deferral plan that also allows employer matching or nonelective contributions.

CHAPTER 10 QUESTIONS FOR REVIEW

1. Each of the following statements is true about a SIMPLE plan EXCEPT

   A. amounts deferred to a SIMPLE account are subject to current income taxation
   B. eligible employers must have 100 or fewer employees
   C. an employer must make a contribution every year to each participating employee's account
   D. amounts in an employee's SIMPLE account are 100 percent vested at all times

2. If an employer with a SIMPLE plan no longer meets the eligibility requirements, it can only continue to maintain its SIMPLE plan for

   A. one more year
   B. two more years
   C. three more years
   D. four more years

3. SIMPLE plans may be structured as

   A. 401(k) plans only
   B. either 401(k) plans or SEPs
   C. both 401(k) plans and Keogh plans
   D. both 401(k) plans and IRAs

4. All of the following statements about contributions to a SIMPLE plan are true EXCEPT

   A. amounts deferred by an employee to a SIMPLE account are subject to Social Security and federal unemployment taxes
   B. no contributions other than employee elective contributions and employer contributions can be made to a SIMPLE account
   C. an employee can choose to defer a flat dollar amount to his or her SIMPLE account each year
   D. an employer can make a nonelective contribution of 2 percent of compensation for each eligible employee

5. Whom of the following must receive a notice specifying the contribution alternative selected by the employer and a summary of the employee's rights under the SIMPLE plan?

   A. Employees only
   B. Employees and the Secretary of the Treasury
   C. Employees and the trustee
   D. Employees, the trustee and the Secretary of the Treasury

Appendix A
Sample 401(k) Plan

Permissions and Disclaimer

This Appendix contains a sample 401(k) plan that is representative of a typical 401(k) plan. It is reprinted by permission of Tax Management Inc., a subsidiary of the Bureau of National Affairs Inc., Washington, DC. This plan is not intended to be accepted as the final word in either a legal or a technical sense. It is included for illustrative purposes only.

Article I. Introduction.

1.01. Purpose of Plan. ABC Company, Inc. has established this Plan to encourage savings by its employees for their retirement.

1.02. Plan and Trust intended to qualify. This Plan and its related Trust are intended to qualify as a profit-sharing plan and trust under Code §401(a), and the cash or deferred arrangement forming part of the Plan is intended to qualify under Code §401(k). Subject to the provisions of §§5.06, 13.03, and 13.05, no part of the corpus or income of the Trust forming part of the Plan will be used for or diverted to purposes other than for the exclusive purpose of providing benefits to Participants and Beneficiaries.

Article II. Definitions.

Wherever used herein, a pronoun or adjective in the masculine gender includes the feminine gender, the singular includes the plural, and the following terms have the following meanings unless a different meaning is clearly required by the context:

2.01. "Accounts" mean, for any Participant, his After Tax Contribution Account and his Tax Deferred Contribution Account.

2.02. "Administrator" means the Company or other person appointed to administer the Plan in accordance with Article III.

2.03. "Affiliated Company" means (a) any corporation (other than the Company) that is a member of a controlled group of corporations (as defined in §414(b) of the Code) of which the Company is also a member, (b) any trade or business (other than the Company), whether or not incorporated, that is under common control (as defined in §414(c) of the Code) with the Company, and (c) any trade or business (other than the Company) that is a member of an affiliated service group (as defined in §414(m) of the Code) of which the Company is also a member; provided, that the term "Affiliated Company" shall not include any corporation or unincorporated trade or business prior to the date on which such corporation, trade or business satisfies the affiliation or control tests of (a), (b) or (c) above. In identifying any "Affiliated Companies" for purposes of §7.03, the definitions in §§414(b) and (c) of the Code shall be modified as provided in §415(h) of the Code.

2.04. "After Tax Contribution Account" means, for any Participant, the account described in §7.01 to which the Participant's After Tax Contributions are credited.

2.05. "After Tax Contribution" means a contribution made by a Participant under §5.07.

2.06. "Annual Addition" means, in the case of any Participant, the sum for any Limitation Year of the Elective Contribution, Matching Contribution, and any Special Contribution made for the Participant's benefit for such Year, plus any After Tax Contributions of the Participant for such Year.

2.07. "Beneficiary" means any person entitled under §8.03 to receive benefits under the Plan upon the death of the Participant.

2.08. "Board of Directors" means the Board of Directors of the Company. The Board of Directors may allocate or delegate its fiduciary responsibilities, or may designate others to carry out its fiduciary responsibilities, in writing in accordance with ERISA §405.

2.09. "Bonus" means the amount awarded to a Participant for a Plan Year under the Company's annual bonus program, including the amount contributed to this Plan as an Elective Contribution.

2.10. "Code" means the Internal Revenue Code of 1986, as amended from time to time. Reference to any section or subsection of the Code includes reference to any comparable or succeeding provisions of any legislation which amends, supplements or replaces such section or subsection.

2.11. **"Company"** means ABC Company, Inc., a [State] corporation, and any successor to all or a major portion of its assets or business which assumes the obligations of the Company with the consent of the Trustees.

2.12. **"Computation Period"** means, for any Employee, a period of 12 consecutive months beginning with the Employee's Employment Commencement Date and each anniversary of that Date.

2.13. **"Effective Date"** means: ____________.

2.14(a). **"Elective Contribution"** means a contribution made for the benefit of a Participant under §5.01.

(b). **"Elective Deferrals"** means any employer contributions made to the plan at the election of the Participant, in lieu of cash compensation, and shall include contributions made pursuant to a salary reduction agreement or other deferral mechanism. With respect to any taxable year, a Participant's Elective Deferral is the sum of all employer contributions made on behalf of such Participant pursuant to an election to defer under any qualified CODA as described in Code §401(k), any simplified employee pension cash or deferred arrangement as described in Code §402(h)(1)(B), any eligible deferred compensation plan within the meaning of Code §457, any plan described in Code §501(c)(18), and any employer contributions made on the behalf of a participant for the purchase of an annuity contract under Code §403(b) pursuant to a salary reduction agreement. Elective Deferrals shall not include any deferrals properly distributed as excess annual additions.

(c). **"Excess Elective Deferrals"** shall mean those Elective Deferrals that are includible in a Participant's gross income under Code §402(g) to the extent such Participant's Elective Deferrals for a taxable year exceed the dollar limitation for the year under §402(g). Excess Elective Deferrals shall be treated as annual additions under the plan, unless such amounts are distributed no later than the first April 15 following the close of the participant's taxable year.

2.15. **"Employee"** means any individual employed by the Company.

2.16. **"Employment Commencement Date"** means the first day on which the Employee performs an Hour of Service.

2.17. **"ERISA"** means the Employee Retirement Income Security Act of 1974, as from time to time amended, and any successor statute or statutes of similar import.

2.18. **"Highly Compensated Employee"** means an employee of the Company or any Affiliated Company who, during the Plan Year in question or the preceding Plan Year: (a) was at any time a 5% owner (as defined in Code §416(i)(1)) of the Company or any Affiliated Company; (b) received Total Compensation in excess of $75,000; (c) received Total Compensation in excess of $50,000 and was in the top-paid group of employees (as defined in Code §414(q), based upon the exclusion of all employees excludible under §414(q)(8)) for the Year, or (d) was at any time an officer of the Company or any Affiliated Company and received Total Compensation greater than 50% of the defined benefit plan dollar limitation described in Code §415(b)(1)(A). The $75,000 and $50,000 amounts in (b) and (c) above shall automatically be adjusted if and to the extent the corresponding amounts in Code §414(q) are adjusted by the Secretary of the Treasury. No more than 50 employees of the Company and any Affiliated Companies (or, if less, the greater of three employees or 10% of all employees of the Company and any Affiliated Companies) shall be treated as officers for purposes of clause (d) above. An individual who was not described in (a), (b), (c), or (d) above during the preceding Plan Year shall be a Highly Compensated Employee during the current Plan Year only if he is described in (a) above or is among the 100 employees of the Company and any Affiliated Companies with the greatest Total Compensation for the current Plan Year.

2.19. "Highly Compensated Participant" means a Participant who is a Highly Compensated Employee.

2.20. "Hour of Service" means:

(a) each hour for which the Employee is directly or indirectly paid, or entitled to payment, for the performance of duties for the Company or any Affiliated Company, each such hour to be credited to the Employee for the Computation Period in which the duties were performed;

(b) each hour for which the Employee is directly or indirectly paid, or entitled to payment, by the Company or any Affiliated Company (including payments made or due from a trust fund or insurer to which the Company or any Affiliated Company contributes or pays premiums) on account of a period of time during which no duties are performed (irrespective of whether the employment relationship has terminated) due to vacation, holiday, illness, incapacity, disability, layoff, jury duty, military duty, or leave of absence, each such hour to be credited to the Employee for the Computation Period in which such period of time occurs, subject to the following rules:

(1) No more than 501 Hours of Service will be credited under this subsection (b) to the Employee on account of any single continuous period during which the Employee performs no duties;

(2) Hours of Service will not be credited under this subsection (b) for a payment which solely reimburses an individual for medically related expenses, or which is made or due under a plan maintained solely for the purpose of complying with applicable workers' compensation, unemployment compensation or disability insurance laws;

(3) If the period during which the Employee performs no duties falls within two or more Computation Periods and if the payment made on account of such period is not calculated on the basis of units of time, the Hours of Service credited with respect to such period shall be allocated between not more than the first two such Computation Periods on any reasonable basis consistently applied with respect to similarly situated Employees;

(c) each hour not credited under (a) or (b) above for which back pay, irrespective of mitigation of damages, has been either awarded or agreed to by the Company or any Affiliated Company, each such hour to be credited to the Employee for the Computation Period to which the award or agreement pertains; and

(d) each noncompensated hour during a period of leave of absence from the Company or any Affiliated Company for service in the armed forces of the United States if the Employee returns to work for the Company or any Affiliated Company at a time when he has reemployment rights under federal law.

Hours of Service to be credited to an individual under (a), (b) and (c) above will be calculated and credited pursuant to 29 C.F.R. §2530.200(b)-2(b) and (c), which are incorporated herein by reference. Hours of Service to be credited to an individual during an absence described in (d) above will be determined by the Administrator with reference to the individual's most recent normal work schedule. If the Administrator cannot so determine the number of Hours to be credited, there shall instead be credited eight Hours of Service for each day of absence.

2.21. **"Limitation Year"** means the Plan Year.

2.22. **"Matching Contribution"** means a contribution made for the benefit of a Participant under §5.02.

2.23. **"Normal Retirement Date"** means the date on which the Participant attains age 65.

2.24. **"Participant"** means each Employee who participates in the Plan in accordance with Article IV.

2 25. **"Plan"** means the ABC Company, Inc. Savings Incentive Plan set forth therein, together with any and all amendments and supplements hereto.

2.26. **"Plan Year"** means the 12-month period ending December 31 of each year.

2.27. **"Qualified Domestic Relations Order"** means any judgment, decree or order (including approval of a property settlement agreement) which: (a) relates to the provision of child support, alimony payments, or marital property rights to a spouse, former spouse, child or other dependent of a Participant; (b) is made pursuant to a State domestic relations law (including a community property law); and (c) constitutes a qualified domestic relations order within the meaning of Code §414(p).

2.28. **"Special Contribution"** means any contribution made for the benefit of a participant under §5.03.

2.29. **"Tax Deferred Contribution Account"** means, for any Participant, the account described in §7.01 to which Elective Contributions, Matching Contributions, and any Special Contributions for the Participant's benefit are credited.

2.30. "Taxable Compensation" means, in the case of each Participant and for each Plan Year, the Participant's wages, salaries, fees for professional services and other amounts payable for personal services actually rendered during the Plan Year in the course of employment with the Company and any Affiliated Companies, but does not include Elective, Matching or Special Contributions or other amounts which are excluded under the definition of compensation in the Treasury Regulations promulgated under Code §415. In no event shall the amount of a Participant's Taxable Compensation taken into account under the Plan for any Plan Year exceed $150,000 (or such larger amount as the Secretary of the Treasury may determine for such Plan Year under Code §401(a)(17)).

2.31. "Total Compensation" means, in the case of each Participant and for each Plan Year, all compensation payable to the Participant by the Company and any Affiliated Companies for services rendered during the Plan Year, including salary and Bonus for the Plan Year, overtime pay, and any other compensation payable for the Plan Year, and including any Elective Contributions or other amounts that would have been paid to the Participant for the Plan Year but for any election under Code §§125, 401(k), 402(h), or 403(b). Subject to the foregoing, "Total Compensation" does not include any contributions under this Plan or any other employee benefit plan, fund, program or arrangement, whether now or hereafter established. In no event shall a Participant's Total Compensation for any Plan Year exceed, for purposes of this Plan, $150,000 (or such larger amount as the Secretary of the Treasury may determine for such Plan Year under Code §401(a)(17)).

2.32. "Trust" means the trust established between the Company and the Trustee in connection with the Plan.

2.33. "Trust Fund" means the property held in trust by the Trustees for the benefit of Participants, former Participants and their Beneficiaries.

2.34. "Trustees" means the persons appointed as Trustees pursuant to §6.01, any successor trustee or trustees, and any additional trustee or trustees.

2.35. "Valuation Date" means the last day of the Plan Year and such other day or days as the Administrator may determine.

2.36. "Year of Service" means, with respect to any Employee, a Computation Period during which the Employee has completed 1,000 or more Hours of Service.

Article III. Administration.

3.01. Administrator.

(a) In general. The Plan will be administered by the Company or by any person, including a committee consisting of at least three individuals, but not more than five, appointed from time to time by the Board of Directors to serve at its pleasure. Participants may be appointed to serve as Administrator at the discretion of the Board of Directors. Except as may be directed by the Company, no person serving as Administrator will receive any compensation for his services as Administrator.

(b) Actions by committee. If a committee is appointed to serve as Administrator, it will act by majority vote. If at any time a majority of the individuals serving on such committee and eligible to vote are unable to agree, or if there is only one such individual, any action required of the committee will be taken by the Board of Directors and its decision will be final. An individual serving on such committee who is a Participant will not vote or act on any matter relating solely to himself.

3.02. Powers of Administrator. The Administrator will have full power to administer the Plan in all of its details, subject, however, to the requirements of ERISA. For this purpose the Administrator's power will include, but will not be limited to, the following authority:

(a) to make and enforce such rules and regulations as it deems necessary or proper for the efficient administration of the Plan or required to comply with applicable law;

(b) to interpret the Plan, its interpretation thereof in good faith to be final and conclusive on any Employee, former Employee, Participant, former Participant and Beneficiary;

(c) to decide all questions concerning the Plan and the eligibility of any person to participate in the Plan;

(d) to compute the amounts to be distributed to any Participant, former Participant or Beneficiary in accordance with the provisions of the Plan, and to determine the person or persons to whom such amounts will be distributed;

(e) to authorize the payment of distributions;

(f) to keep such records and submit such filings, elections, applications, returns or other documents or forms as may be required under the Code and applicable regulations, or under other federal, state or local law and regulations;

(g) to appoint such agents, counsel, accountants and consultants as may be required to assist in administering the Plan; and

(h) by written instrument, to allocate and delegate its fiduciary responsibilities in accordance with §405 of ERISA.

3.03. Examination of records. The Administrator will make available to each Participant such of its records as pertain to him, for examination at reasonable times during normal business hours.

3.04. Nondiscriminatory exercise of authority. Whenever, in the administration of the Plan, any discretionary action by the Administrator is required, the Administrator shall exercise its authority in a nondiscriminatory manner so that all persons similarly situated will receive substantially the same treatment.

3.05. Reliance on tables, etc. In administering the Plan, the Administrator will be entitled, to the extent permitted by law, to rely conclusively on all tables, valuations, certificates, opinions and reports which are furnished by any accountant, trustee, counsel or other expert who is employed or engaged by the Administrator or by the Company on the Administrator's behalf.

3.06. Named fiduciary. The Administrator will be a "named fiduciary" for purposes of ERISA §402(a)(1) with authority to control and manage the operation and administration of the Plan, and will be responsible for complying with all of the reporting and disclosure requirements of Part I of Subtitle B of Title I of ERISA. The Administrator will not, however, have any authority over the investment of assets of the Trust.

3.07. Claims and review procedures.

(a) Claims procedure. If any person believes he is being denied any rights or benefits under the Plan, such person may file a claim in writing with the Administrator. If any such claim is wholly or partially denied, the Administrator will notify such person of its decision in writing. Such notification will contain (1) specific reasons for the denial, (2) specific reference to pertinent plan provisions, (3) a description of any additional material or information necessary for such person to perfect such claim and an explanation of why such material or information is necessary and (4) information as to the steps to be taken if the person wishes to submit a request for review. Such notification will be given within 90 days after the claim is received by the Administrator (or within 180 days, if special circumstances require an extension of time for processing the claim, and if written notice of such extension and circumstances is given to such person within the initial 90 day period). If such notification is not given within such period, the claim will be considered denied as of the last day of such period and such person may request a review of his claim.

(b) Review procedure. Within 60 days after the date on which a person receives written notice of a denied claim (or, if applicable, within 60 days after the date on which such denial is considered to have occurred) such person (or his duly authorized representative) may (1) file a written request with the Administrator for a review of his denied claim and of pertinent documents and (2) submit written issues and comments to the Administrator. The Administrator will notify such person of its decision in writing. Such notification will be written in a manner calculated to be understood by such person and will contain specific reasons for the decision as well as specific references to pertinent Plan provisions. The decision on review will be made within 60 days after the request for review is received by the Administrator (or within 120 days, if special circumstances require an extension of time for processing the request, such as an election by the Administrator to hold a hearing, and if written notice of such extension and circumstances is given to such person within the initial 60 day period). If the decision on review is not made within such period, the claim will be considered denied.

3.08. Indemnification of Administrator. The Company agrees to indemnify and defend to the fullest extent of the law any Employee or former Employee who serves or has served in the capacity of Administrator or as a member of a committee designated as Administrator against any liabilities, damages, costs and expenses (including attorneys' fees and amounts paid in settlement of any claims approved by the Company) occasioned by any act or omission to act in connection with the Plan, if such act or omission to act is in good faith.

3.09. Costs of Administrator. All reasonable costs and expenses incurred by the Administrator and the Trustees in administering the Plan and Trust will be paid by the Company.

Article IV. Participation.

4.01. Participation. Each Employee will become a Participant on the later of:

(a) the Effective Date; and

(b) the day on which he completes one Year of Service.

4.02. Notice to Participants. The Administrator will inform each Employee who satisfies the requirements of §4.01 above of his eligibility to participate in the Plan.

4.03. Cessation of participation. A Participant will cease to be a Participant as of the earlier of:

(a) the date on which he ceases to be an Employee; or

(b) the date on which the Plan terminates.

4.04. Breaks in participation. If an individual who has ceased to be a Participant pursuant to §4.03(a) again becomes an Employee, he will become a Participant in the Plan on the first day on which he again completes an Hour of Service.

Article V. Contributions.

5.01. Elective Contributions. On or before December 1 of each Plan Year, each Participant (including each Employee who is expected to become a Participant before the end of the Plan Year) may enter into a Bonus deferral agreement with the Company, in a form prescribed or approved by the Administrator, pursuant to which all or part of the Participant's Bonus for the Plan Year will be contributed by the Company to the Trust as an Elective Contribution in lieu of being paid to the Participant in cash. The portion of the Participant's Bonus to be contributed to the Trust shall be specified by the Participant, but shall not exceed the lesser of (a) $7,000 (or such higher limit as may be in effect for the Plan Year under Code §402(g)(1)), reduced by any other elective deferrals (as defined in Code §402(g)(3)) of the Participant through the Company or any Affiliated Company for the same year, or (b) 15% of the Participant's Total Compensation from the Company for the Plan Year. This maximum percentage shall be reduced, if necessary, so that it will not exceed the lowest percentage determined by taking each Participant's Bonus for the Plan Year and dividing it by his Total Compensation for the Plan Year.

5.02. **Matching Contributions**. For each Plan Year the Company shall contribute to the Trust, for the benefit of each Participant for whom an Elective Contribution is made, a Matching Contribution equal to 50% of such portion of the Participant's Elective Contribution as does not exceed 6% of the Participant's Total Compensation from the Company.

5.03. **Special Contributions**. In addition to the Elective Contributions and Matching Contributions for a Plan Year, the Company may, in its discretion, make Special Contributions to the Trust for the benefit of (a) all Participants, or (b) all Participants other than Highly Compensated Participants. For all Participants who benefit from a Special Contribution, the Special Contribution shall be in an amount equal to the same percentage of Total Compensation from the Company.

5.04. **Maximum amount of Company contributions**. In no event will the total contributions to be made under §§5.01, 5.02 and 5.03 for any Plan Year (a) be in an amount which would cause the Annual Addition for any Participant to exceed the amount permitted under §7.03, or (b) exceed the maximum amount deductible under the applicable provisions of the Code. All contributions under the Plan are hereby conditioned on their deductibility under Code §404. In the event the amounts to be contributed for any Participant will cause his Annual Addition to exceed the amount permitted under §7.03, such contributions shall be reduced in the manner and order described in §7.04. In the event the total contributions to be made under this Article V would exceed the limitation described in clause (b) above, the Company shall reduce its Special Contributions, Matching Contributions and Elective Contributions in such order and manner as the Company determines in its discretion, under rules uniformly applicable to similarly situated Participants, with any reductions in Elective Contributions to be paid to the affected Participants in cash.

5.05. **Time for making Company contributions**. All contributions to be made under §§5.01, 5.02 and 5.03 for any Plan Year shall be contributed in cash to the Trust and credited to the Participants' accounts as soon as practicable following the close of such Plan Year, and in all events not later than the time prescribed by law (including extensions thereof) for filing the Company's federal income tax return for its taxable year in or with which such Plan Year ends.

5.06. **Return of Company contributions**. If a contribution to the Trust under §§5.01, 5.02 or 5.03 is (a) made by reason of a good faith mistake of fact, or (b) believed by the Company in good faith to be deductible under Code §404, but the deduction is disallowed, the Trustees shall, upon request by the Company, return to the Company the excess of the amount contributed over the amount, if any, that would have been contributed had there not occurred a mistake of fact or a mistake in determining the deduction. In no event shall the return of a contribution hereunder cause any Participant's Accounts to be reduced to less than they would have been had the mistaken or nondeductible amount not been contributed. No return of a contribution hereunder shall be made more than one year after the mistaken payment of the contribution, or disallowance of the deduction, as the case may be.

5.07. After-Tax Contributions. Any Participant may, at his option, but subject to §§5.08 and 7.03, make cash contributions on an after-tax basis to the Trust in any Plan Year in an amount which is not more than 10% of his Total Compensation from the Company for the Plan Year. After-Tax Contributions may be made at such times and in such manner as the Administrator determines under rules uniformly applicable to similarly situated Participants. Any After-Tax Contributions made by a Participant shall be credited to the Participant's After-Tax Contribution Account.

5.08. Nondiscrimination requirements.

(a) Elective Contributions for any Plan Year must satisfy at least one of the following tests:

(1) The average of the individual ratios of Elective Contributions to Total Compensation (the "deferral ratios") for the Plan Year for all Highly Compensated Participants does not exceed the product of 1.25 and the average of the deferral ratios for all other Participants, or

(2) The excess of the average of the deferral ratios for all Highly Compensated Participants over that for all other Participants does not exceed two percentage points, and the average of the deferral ratios for all Highly Compensated Participants does not exceed twice the average of the deferral ratios for all other Participants, or

(3) Clause (1) or (2) is satisfied after taking into account Matching Contributions and any Special Contributions for the Plan Year, as if they were additional Elective Contributions, in determining each Participant's deferral ratio.

Clause (3) above shall be subject to such conditions as may be prescribed by regulations. Contributions under other plans of the Company or any Affiliated Company may also be taken into account under Clause (3) to the extent permitted by regulations.

(b) Matching Contributions and After-Tax Contributions, taken together, for any Plan Year must satisfy at least one of the following tests:

(1) the average of the individual ratios of (A) Matching Contributions and After-Tax Contributions to (B) Total Compensation (the "contribution ratios") for the Plan Year for all Highly Compensated Participants does not exceed 125% of the average of the contribution ratios for all other Participants, or

(2) The excess of the average of the contribution ratios for all Highly Compensated Participants over that for all other Participants does not exceed two percentage

points, and the average of the contribution ratios for all Highly Compensated Participants does not exceed twice the average of the contribution ratios for all other Participants, or

(3) Clause (1) or (2) is satisfied after taking into account Elective Contributions (to the extent they satisfy §5.08(a)) and any Special Contributions for the Plan Year (other than Special Contributions that need to be taken into account under §5.08(a)(3)) as if they were additional Matching Contributions or After-Tax Contributions, in determining each Participant's contribution ratio.

Clause (2) above shall not apply if and to the extent regulations provide that it cannot apply. Clause (3) above shall be subject to such conditions as may be prescribed by regulations. Contributions under other plans of the Company or any Affiliated Company may also be taken into account under Clause (3) to the extent permitted by regulations.

(c) If any individual employed by the Company or any Affiliated Company is a member of the family (as defined in Code §414(q)(6)(B)) of a Highly Compensated Employee who is either (1) a 5% owner (as defined in Code §416(i)(1)) of the Company or (2) among the 10 individuals receiving the greatest Total Compensation during the Plan Year, such individual shall not be taken into account separately under this §5.08. Instead, the Total Compensation of such individual, any Elective, Matching and Special Contributions made for the individual's benefit, and any After-Tax Contributions by such individual, shall be aggregated with the Total Compensation and Elective, Matching, Special and After-Tax Contributions for the Highly Compensated Employee in applying this §5.08, as if the two individuals were a single individual.

5.09. Adjustments by Administrator.

(a) The Administrator may, in its sole discretion, decrease the amount of the Elective Contribution to be made for the benefit of any Participant, and pay the amount of the decrease to the Participant in cash, if the Administrator deems such a decrease to be necessary to satisfy either the nondiscrimination requirement of §5.08(a) or the limitations described in §5.04, or both. If the Administrator decreases any Elective Contributions to meet the nondiscrimination requirement of §5.08(a), such decrease shall be made first in the Elective Contributions for the Highly Compensated Participants whose Elective Contributions represent the highest percentage of Total Compensation, so that no reduction is made in the Elective Contribution for any Highly Compensated Participant as long as any other Highly Compensated Participant has a higher percentage of Elective Contribution to Total Compensation. Any decrease in the Elective Contribution for a Participant will also be effective for purposes of determining the amount of the Matching Contribution to be made for the Participant's benefit under §5.02.

(b) The Administrator may, in its sole discretion, decrease the amount of After-Tax Contributions, if any, and Matching Contributions to be made for the benefit of Highly Compensated Participants if the Administrator deems such decrease to be necessary to satisfy the nondiscrimination requirement of §5.08(b). Any such decrease shall be made only after any adjustments under §5.09(a) or §7.04 have been made. The Administrator shall first decrease the amount of any After-Tax Contributions to be made for the Plan Year, and then refund any After-Tax Contributions already made for the Plan Year, before decreasing any Matching Contributions under this §5.09(b). Any decrease in Matching Contributions to satisfy §5.08(b) shall be made first in the Matching Contributions for the Highly Compensated Participants whose Matching Contributions represent the highest percentage of Total Compensation, so that no reduction is made in the Matching Contribution for any Highly Compensated Participant as long as any other Highly Compensated Participant had a higher percentage of Matching Contribution to Total Compensation. If Elective Contributions are taken into account under §5.08(b)(3) to satisfy either §5.08(b)(1) or §5.08(b)(2), then such Elective Contributions shall be proportionately reduced along with the Matching Contributions to the extent the Administrator deems necessary to satisfy §5.08(b)(3).

5.10. Distribution of excess contributions. If, after all contributions for a Plan Year have been made, the nondiscrimination requirements of §5.08 have not been satisfied for the Plan Year, the Administrator shall, as soon as practicable (but in no event later than the close of the following Plan Year), distribute the excess contributions (plus any income and minus any loss allocable to such excess) to Highly Compensated Participants in accordance with Code §§401(k)(8) and 401(m)(6), to the extent necessary to satisfy §5.08. Except to the extent otherwise required by regulations, any distribution to a Participant under Code §401(m)(6) shall be deemed a distribution, first, of the Participant's After-Tax Contributions (if any) for the Plan Year and any income allocable to such contributions, and then a distribution of Matching Contributions and income allocable to such contributions. If there has been a net investment loss instead of income allocable to excess contributions, the amount of excess contributions to be distributed hereunder shall be reduced by such loss to the extent permitted by Code §§401(k)(8) or 401(m)(6) or regulations thereunder.

5.11. Distribution of excess elective deferrals. If, on or before March 1 of any year, a Participant notifies the Administrator, in accordance with Code §402(g)(2)(A) and regulations thereunder, that all or a specified part of an elective Contribution made or to be made for his benefit represents an excess Elective Deferral for the preceding taxable year of the Participant, the Administrator shall make every reasonable effort to cause such excess Elective Deferral and any earnings thereon, to be distributed to the Participant no later than the April 15 following such notification. If the Participant's Elective Contribution has not yet been contributed to the Trust, the Elective Contribution shall be reduced by the amount of the excess Elective Deferral and such amount shall be paid to the Participant in cash. Except to the extent otherwise provided in regulations, any amount paid to the Trust and distributed under this §5.11 shall be taken into account in applying §§5.08, 5.09 and 5.10 as if it had not been distributed, except that any decrease in the Elective Contribution for a Participant under §5.09 or distribution of an excess Elective Contribution to a Participant under §5.10 shall be reduced by the amount of any distribution to the Participant under this §5.11. For purposes of this §5.11, the Administrator shall be deemed to have been notified of an excess deferral if such excess deferral arises solely from elective deferrals made under the plan or plans of this Employer.

Article VI. Trust Fund.

6.01. Appointment of Trustees. The Board of Directors shall appoint one or more individuals or corporations to act as Trustees under the Plan, and at any time may remove and appoint a successor to any such person or persons. The Company may enter into a trust agreement with the Trustees and make such amendments to such trust agreement or such further agreements as the Company in its sole discretion may deem necessary or desirable to carry out the Plan.

6.02. Investment of the Trust Fund. All contributions to the Trust for a Participant's benefit shall be held by the Trustees in the Trust Fund and invested by the Trustees solely in accordance with the instructions of the Participant. The Participant shall exercise exclusive control over the investment of his Accounts, and the Trustees shall have no liability for any such investment or for following any such instruction by the Participant. No Participant shall, however, direct any investment that would constitute a "prohibited transaction" within the meaning of ERISA §406, unless covered by a statutory or administrative exemption to §406, or that would violate any other provision of ERISA, nor may a Participant direct that any part of his Accounts be loaned to the Participant except as permitted by Article X. Upon death or other termination of employment of a Participant, the Participant's accounts shall thereafter be invested in the sole discretion of the Trustees in savings accounts, certificates of deposit, U.S. Government obligations of five years or less, money market instruments, or mutual funds investing predominantly in one or more of the foregoing.

Article VII. Participant Accounts.

7.01. Accounts. The Trustees shall maintain on their books for each Participant a Tax Deferred Contribution Account and an After-Tax Contribution Account, together with such other accounts and sub-accounts as the Trustees in their discretion deem appropriate.

7.02. Adjustment of accounts. With respect to the Accounts required by §7.01, the Trustees shall, as of each Valuation Date:

(a) First, reduce the balance of each Participant's Tax Deferred Contribution Account and After-Tax Contribution Account by the aggregate amount of all distributions or withdrawals made from each such Account since the preceding Valuation Date;

(b) Second, adjust the balance of each Participant's Tax Deferred Contribution Account and After-Tax Contribution Account to reflect the current fair market value of the assets in which such Accounts are invested;

(c) Third, credit the After-Tax Contribution Account of each Participant with the amount of After-Tax Contributions, if any, made by the Participant since the preceding Valuation Date; and

(d) Fourth, in the case of the last Valuation Date of each Plan Year, credit each Participant's Tax Deferred Contribution Account with any Elective Contribution, Matching Contribution and Special Contribution made for the benefit of the Participant for such Plan Year.

For purposes of this §7.02, the word "Participant" shall include a former Participant if amounts remain credited to one or more of his Accounts.

7.03. Limitations. Notwithstanding any other provisions of the Plan, the Annual Addition to a Participant's accounts under the Plan for any Limitation Year, when added to the annual additions to his accounts for such Year under all other defined contribution plans maintained by the Company or any Affiliated Company, shall not exceed the lesser of (a) $30,000 (or, if greater, one-fourth of the limitation in effect for the Limitation Year under §415(b)(1)(A) of the Code), or (b) 25% of the Participant's Taxable Compensation for such Limitation Year. In the case of a Participant who also participates in a defined benefit plan maintained by the Company or an Affiliated Company, the Annual Addition for a Limitation Year will, if necessary, be further limited so that the sum of the Participant's "defined contribution fraction" (as determined under Code §415(e) and the regulations thereunder, including any special transition rules) and his "defined benefit plan fraction" (as determined under Code §415(e) and the regulations thereunder) for such Limitation Year does not exceed 1.0. In determining such fractions, 1.0 shall replace 1.25 each time it appears in Code §415(e), unless the requirements of Code §416(h)(2) are satisfied.

7.04. Order of adjustments to satisfy limitations. To the extent necessary to satisfy the limitations of §7.03 for any Participant, the Participant's Annual Addition under this Plan shall be reduced before any reduction in his annual addition under any other defined contribution plan or his benefit under any defined benefit plan. The Participant's Annual Addition under this Plan shall be reduced, first, by reducing and refunding to him his After-Tax Contributions, if any, for the Limitation Year, to the extent such reduction has the effect of reducing his Annual Addition. If further adjustments are necessary, the Participant's Elective Contribution for the Limitation Year shall be reduced, along with any Matching Contribution based upon the reduced portion of such Elective Contribution. If further adjustments are required, the Special Contribution, if any, for the Participant's benefit for the Limitation Year shall be reduced.

Article VIII. Benefits Upon Termination of Employment or Death.

8.01. Vesting. Each Participant will at all times have a fully vested and nonforfeitable interest in his Accounts.

8.02. Retirement or other termination of employment. Each Participant will be eligible for normal retirement upon attaining his Normal Retirement Date. Each Participant will be eligible for early retirement upon attaining age 55. If a Participant retires or ceases to be an Employee for any other reason except death, he shall be entitled under this §8.02 to a benefit equal to the value of his Accounts, subject to §10.06, which shall be distributed in accordance with §§8.04 and 8.05.

8.03. Death.

(a) If a Participant dies before the distribution of his Accounts has been completed under §8.04, upon his death his designated Beneficiary will have a fully vested and nonforfeitable interest in, and will be entitled to receive, the value of his Accounts, subject to §10.06. Distribution to the Beneficiary will be made in accordance with §§8.04 and 8.06.

(b) If a Participant was married at the time of death, he shall be deemed to have designated his surviving spouse as his Beneficiary unless:

(1) prior to his death, he designated as his Beneficiary a person other than his surviving spouse, such designation to be made in writing at such time and in such manner as the Administrator shall approve or prescribe; and

(2) either — (A) his surviving spouse consents in writing to the designation described in (1) above, such consent acknowledges the effect of such designation and the specific non-spouse Beneficiary (including any class of Beneficiaries or any contingent Beneficiaries) or authorizes the Participant to designate Beneficiaries without further consent, and such consent is witnessed by a Plan representative or a notary public, or (B) it is established to the satisfaction of the Administrator that the consent required under (A) above may not be obtained because there is no spouse, because the spouse cannot be located, or because of such other circumstances as the Secretary of the Treasury may prescribe; and

(3) the non-spouse Beneficiary designated in accordance with the provisions of this Section survives the Participant.

Any consent by a spouse under (2)(A) above, or a determination by the Administrator with respect to such spouse under (2)(B) above, shall be effective only with respect to such spouse. Any such consent shall be irrevocable, but shall be effective only with respect to the specific Beneficiary designation unless the consent expressly permits designations by the Participant without any requirement of further consent.

(c) A Participant who is not married may designate a Beneficiary in writing at such time and in such manner as the Administrator shall approve or prescribe.

(d) A Participant who has designated a Beneficiary in accordance with this §8.03 may change such designation at any time by giving written notice to the Administrator, subject to the conditions of this §8.03 and such additional conditions and requirements as the Administrator may prescribe in accordance with applicable law.

(e) If a Participant dies without a surviving Beneficiary, the full amount payable upon his death will be paid to his issue per stirpes. If any of such issue is a minor, the Trustees may deposit his share in a savings account to his credit in a savings bank or other financial institution for the benefit of such issue. If there is no surviving issue, then the amount may be paid to his executor or administrator or applied to the payment of his debts and funeral expenses, all as the Administrator shall determine.

8.04. Form of distributions. Distributions under §8.02 or 8.03 may be paid in cash or in kind, in either or both of the following ways, all as the Participant (or, if §8.03 applies, his Beneficiary) shall elect, subject to §§8.05 and 8.06: (a) in a single payment; or (b) in substantially equal installments over a fixed period not to exceed the life expectancy of the Participant or the joint life and last survivor expectancy of the Participant and his Beneficiary. If distributions are being made pursuant to §8.03, the fixed period shall not exceed the life expectancy of the Beneficiary.

If the Participant's Beneficiary is not his spouse, the present value of the installments payable to the Participant, determined at the time installments commence, shall in all cases be greater than 50% of the present value of all installments to be paid.

8.05. Time of distributions: termination of employment.

(a) In general. Distributions to a Participant under §8.02 will be made or commence not later than the 60th day after the close of the Plan Year in which the Participant's employment terminated, unless the distributee elects in writing to have distributions commence at a later time. The foregoing is subject to the special rules described in (b) and (c), below.

(b) Distributions must commence by age 70½. Notwithstanding any election to the contrary, payment of benefits to a Participant shall commence not later than the April 1 of the calendar year following the calendar year in which the Participant attains age 70½ and shall be made in accordance with the requirements of the minimum required distribution rules of Code §401 (a)(9) and the regulations thereunder.

(c) Cash-out restrictions. No distribution shall be made to a Participant before his Normal Retirement Date unless — (1) the Participant's prior written consent to the distribution has been obtained by the Administrator, (2) the value of the Participant's Accounts does not exceed $3,500, or (3) such distribution is made in accordance with the requirements of applicable law, including the minimum required distribution rules of Code §401(a)(9) and the regulations thereunder.

If the Participant's consent is required under this §8.05(c) but is not provided prior to the time distributions are to be made under the first sentence of this §8.05, distribution shall be made or commence within 60 days after the earliest of (1) the Participant's Normal Retirement Date, (2) the date the Administrator is notified of the Participant's death or (3) the date the Administrator receives from the Participant a written request for distribution.

8.06. Time of distributions — death. Distributions shall be made or commence not later than one year after the Participant's death. In addition, the following special rules apply:

(a) If a Participant dies before the date described in §8.05(a), distributions must either — (1) be made in their entirety within five years after the Participant's death, or (2) be made over a period not extending beyond the recipient's life expectancy.

(b) If a Participant dies after the date described in §8.05(a) and after distribution of his benefits has commenced, but before such distribution has been completed, the remaining benefits shall be distributed at least as rapidly as under the method of distribution under which the Participant was receiving his benefits as of the date of his death.

8.07. Former Participants. For purposes of this Article VIII, the term "Participant" shall include a former Participant.

8.08. Direct rollovers.

(a) Applicability of section. This §8.08 applies to distributions made after 1992. Notwithstanding any other plan provision that would otherwise limit a distributee's election under this §8.08, a distributee may elect, at the time and in the manner prescribed by the Plan Administrator, to have any part of an eligible rollover distribution paid directly to an eligible retirement plan specified by the distributee in a direct rollover.

(b) Definitions.

(1) *Eligible Rollover Distribution* shall mean any distribution of all or any part of the balance to the Distributee's credit, except: (i) a distribution that is one of a series of substantially equal periodic payments (no less frequently than annually) made for the life (or life expectancy) of the Distributee or the joint lives (or joint life expectancies) of the Distributee and his or her designated beneficiary, or for a specified period of 10 years or more; (ii) to the extent that the distribution is required under Code §401(a)(9); and (iii) to the extent that it represents the portion of any distribution that is not includible in gross income (determined without regard to the exclusion for net unrealized appreciation on employer securities).

(2) *Eligible Retirement Plan* shall mean a Code §408(a) individual retirement account, §408(b) individual retirement annuity, §403(a) annuity plan, or an §401(a) qualified retirement plan that accepts the Distributee's Eligible Rollover Distribution. In the case of an Eligible Rollover Distribution to the Participant's surviving spouse, however, an Eligible Retirement Plan is only an individual retirement account or individual retirement annuity.

(3) *Distributee* shall include an Employee or former Employee. The Employee's or former Employee's surviving spouse and the Employee's or former Employee's spouse or former spouse who is the alternate payee under a Qualified Domestic Relations Order, as defined in Code §414(p), also are Distributees with respect to the interest of the spouse or former spouse.

(4) *Direct Rollover* shall mean a payment by the Plan to the Eligible Retirement Plan specified by the Distributee.

Article IX. In-Service Withdrawals.

9.01. Withdrawal of After-Tax Contributions. A Participant may request a withdrawal from his After-Tax Contribution Account at any time and for any reason, up to the full value of such account at the time of the withdrawal, less any portion of such Account which has been loaned to the Participant under Article X.

9.02. Hardship withdrawals.

(a) In General. Any Participant who suffers a financial hardship, as defined in this §9.02, may request a withdrawal from his Accounts, less any portion thereof which has been loaned to the Participant under Article X. Such request shall be made by written notice to the Administrator setting forth the amount requested and the facts establishing the existence of such hardship. Upon receipt of such a request, the Administrator shall determine whether a financial hardship exists; if the Administrator determines that such a hardship does exist, it shall further determine what portion of the amount requested by the Participant is required to meet the need created by the hardship, and shall direct the Trustee to distribute to the Participant the amount so determined to be required. For purposes of this Section, the term "financial hardship" includes any immediate and heavy financial need arising from:

(1) payment of tuition and related educational fees for the next 12 months of post secondary education for the Employee, the Employee's spouse, children or dependents;

(2) the purchase of a primary residence for the Participant (not including regular mortgage payments);

(3) major medical expenses of the Participant, the Participant's spouse or the Participant's dependent or a dependent which are not covered by insurance and which are described in Code §213(d); or

(4) the need to prevent the eviction of the Employee from, or a foreclosure on the mortgage of, the Employee's principal residence.

(b) Additional Restrictions. A distribution will be considered as necessary to satisfy an immediate and heavy financial need of the employee only if:

(1) The Employee has obtained all distributions, other than hardship distributions, and all nontaxable loans under all plans maintained by the employer;

(2) All plans maintained by the employer provide that the employee's Elective Deferrals (and Employee Contributions) will be suspended for 12 months after the receipt of the hardship distribution;

(3) The distribution is not in excess of the amount of an immediate and heavy financial need (including amounts necessary to pay any federal, state or local income taxes or penalties reasonably anticipated to result from the distribution); and

(4) All plans maintained by the employer provide that the employee may not make Elective Deferrals for the employee's taxable year immediately following the taxable year of the hardship distribution in excess of the applicable limit under Code §402(g) for such taxable year less the amount of such Employee's Elective Deferrals for the taxable year of the hardship distribution.

Further, the Administrator may, in its sole discretion, alter the foregoing definition of financial hardship or otherwise limit the amount, time or manner of any distribution under this Section to the extent deemed necessary by the Administrator to satisfy the requirements of Code §401(k) or the regulations thereunder. No distribution under this §9.02 shall be made after December 31, 1988, from any income allocable to Elective Contributions (or, to the extent provided in regulations, from any Matching or Special Contributions or income allocable thereto).

9.03. Withdrawals after age 59½. Any Participant who has attained age 59½ may request a withdrawal of all or part of his interest in his Accounts, less any portion thereof which has been loaned to the Participant under Article X. Such request may be made, whether or not the Participant has suffered a financial hardship, by written notice to the Administrator.

9.04. Subsequent distributions. A withdrawal pursuant to this Article IX will not affect the Participant's right to request or receive distribution of the remaining portion of his Accounts pursuant to Article VIII.

Article X. Loans to Participants.

10.01. Requests by Participants. Upon the written request of a Participant on a form approved or prescribed by the Administrator, the Administrator may direct the Trustees to make a loan from the Trust to such Participant, subject to the conditions described in this Article X.

10.02. Rules and procedures. The Administrator shall determine the time or times each year when loans shall be made available to Participants, and shall formulate such rules and procedures as it deems appropriate relating to such loans.

10.03. Maximum amount of loan. The amount of any loan, together with the aggregate amount of principal and accrued interest owed by the Participant with respect to any prior loans from qualified retirement plans of the Company and any Affiliated Companies, shall not exceed the least of:

(a) $50,000, reduced by the excess of (1) the highest outstanding loan balance of the Participant from such plans during the one year period ending on the day before the loan is made, over (2) the Participant's outstanding loan balance from such plans immediately prior to the loan;

(b) the greater of $10,000 or one-half of the sum of (i) the Participant's Accounts plus (ii) the present value of the Participant's nonforfeitable accrued benefit under other qualified retirement plans of the Company and any Affiliated Companies; or

(c) Ninety percent of the Participant's Accounts. For purposes of this §10.03, the value of a Participant's Accounts shall be determined as of the Valuation Date immediately preceding the date of the loan, and the present value of the Participant's nonforfeitable accrued benefit under any other plan shall be determined by the Administrator in such manner and as of such time as the Administrator decides.

10.04. Note; security; interest. Each loan must be evidenced by a note and must be secured by the Participant's Accounts and by such other security, if any, as the Administrator may require. The loan shall bear interest at a reasonable rate determined by the Administrator.

10.05. Repayment. Each such loan shall be repayable by payroll deduction over a specified period of time, as determined by the Administrator, and on the basis of substantially level payments made no less frequently than quarterly. Such period of time shall not exceed five years unless the loan is used to acquire a dwelling unit which is to be used within a reasonable time as a principal residence of the Participant.

10.06. Repayment upon distribution. If, at the time benefits are to be distributed (or to commence being distributed) to a Participant or his Beneficiary under Article VIII of the Plan, there remains any unpaid balance of a loan hereunder, such unpaid balance shall become immediately due and payable in full. Such unpaid balance, together with any accrued but unpaid interest on the loan, shall be deducted from the Participant's Accounts before any such distribution of benefits is made.

10.07. Note as Trust asset. A note evidencing a loan to a Participant under this Article X shall be an asset of the Trust which is allocated to the account of the Participant, and shall for purposes of the Plan be deemed to have a fair market value at any given time equal to the unpaid balance of the note plus the amount of any accrued but unpaid interest.

10.08. Adjustment of accounts. The amount of any loan made pursuant to this Article X or of any repayment thereof shall be charged or credited to the Participant's Accounts in accordance with procedures to be established by the Administrator.

10.09. Nondiscrimination. Loans shall be made available to all Participants on a reasonably equivalent basis, except that the Administrator may make reasonable distinctions based upon creditworthiness, other obligations of the Participant, state law restrictions affecting payroll deductions and other factors that may adversely affect the ability to assure repayment through payroll deduction. The Administrator may reduce or refuse a requested loan where it determines that timely repayment of the loan through payroll deduction is not assured.

Article XI. Amendment and Termination.

11.01. Amendment. The Company reserves the power at any time or times to amend the provisions of the Plan and Trust to any extent and in any manner that it may deem advisable by delivery to the Trustees of a written instrument executed by the Company providing for such amendment. Upon the delivery of such instrument to the Trustees, such instrument will become effective in accordance with its terms as to all Participants and all persons having or claiming any interest hereunder; provided, however, that the Company will not have the power:

(a) to amend the Plan or Trust in such manner as would cause or permit any part of the assets of the Trust to be diverted to purposes other than for the exclusive benefit of each Participant and his Beneficiary (except as permitted by §§5.06, 13.03, and 13.05), unless such amendment is permitted by law, governmental regulation or ruling;

(b) to amend the Plan or Trust retroactively in such a manner as would deprive any Participant of any benefit to which he was entitled under the Plan by reason of contributions made prior to the amendment, unless such amendment is necessary to conform the Plan or Trust to, or satisfy the conditions of, any law, governmental regulation or ruling, or to permit the Trust and the Plan to meet the requirements of §§401(a) and 501(a) of the Code; or

(c) to amend the Plan or Trust in such manner as would increase the duties or liabilities of the Trustees or affect their fee for services hereunder, unless the Trustees consent thereto in writing.

11.02. Termination. The Company has established the Plan and authorized the establishment of the Trust with the bona fide intention and expectation that contributions will be continued indefinitely, but the Company will have no obligation or liability whatsoever to maintain the Plan for any given length of time and may discontinue contributions under the Plan or terminate the Plan at any time by written notice delivered to the Trustees without liability whatsoever for any such discontinuance or termination. The Plan will be deemed terminated (a) if and when the Company is judicially declared bankrupt, (b) if and when the Company is a party to a merger in which it is not the surviving corporation or sells all or substantially all of its assets, unless the surviving corporation or the purchaser adopts the Plan by an instrument in writing delivered to the Trustees within 60 days after the merger or sale, or (c) upon dissolution of the Company.

11.03. Distributions upon termination of the Plan. Upon termination or partial termination of the Plan or complete discontinuance of contributions thereunder, each Participant will continue to have a fully vested and nonforfeitable interest in his Accounts. Upon termination of the Plan, the Trustees will distribute to each Participant (or other person entitled to distribution) the value of the Participant's Accounts in a single lump sum payment. However, if a successor plan is established within the meaning of Code §401(k)(2)(B)(i)(II), Accounts shall be distributed to Participants and their beneficiaries only in accordance with Articles VIII and IX. Upon the completion of distributions to all Participants, the Trust will terminate, the Trustees will be relieved from all liability under the Trust, and no Participant or other person will have any claims thereunder, except as required by applicable law.

11.04. Merger or consolidation of Plan; transfer of Plan assets. In case of any merger or consolidation of the Plan with, or transfer of assets and liabilities of the Plan to, any other plan, provision must be made so that each Participant would, if the Plan then terminated, receive a benefit immediately after the merger, consolidation or transfer which is equal to or greater than the benefit he would have been entitled to receive immediately before the merger, consolidation or transfer if the Plan had then terminated.

Article XII. Top-Heavy Provisions.

12.01. In General. If the plan is or becomes top-heavy in any plan year beginning after December 31, 1983, the provisions of this Article XII will supersede any conflicting provisions in the plan or adoption agreement.

12.02. Top-heavy definitions. For purposes of this article, the following terms shall have the definitions set forth below:

(a) **Key Employee**: Any employee or former Employee (and the beneficiaries of such Employee) who at any time during the determination period was an officer of the Company if such individual's annual compensation exceeds 50% of the dollar limitation under Code §415(b)(1)(A), an owner (or considered an owner under Code §318) of one of the 10 largest interests in the Company if such individual's compensation exceeds 100% of the dollar limitation under Code §415(c)(1)(A), a 5% owner of the Company, or a 1% owner of the Company who has an annual compensation of more than $150,000. Annual compensation means taxable compensation as defined in §2.30, but including amounts contributed by the employer pursuant to a salary reduction agreement which are excludable from the employee's gross income under §125, §402(e)(3), §402(h)(1)(B) or §403(b) of the Code. The determination period is the plan year containing the Determination Date and the four preceding plan years. The determination of who is a Key Employee will be made in accordance with Code §416(i)(1) and the regulations thereunder.

(b) Top-Heavy Plan: For any plan year beginning after December 31, 1983, this plan is top-heavy if any of the following conditions exists:

(1) If the Top-Heavy Ratio for this plan exceeds 60% and this plan is not part of any Required Aggregation Group or Permissive Aggregation Group of plans.

(2) If this plan is a part of a Required Aggregation Group of plans but not part of a Permissive Aggregation Group and the Top-Heavy Ratio for the group of plans exceeds 60%.

(3) If this plan is a part of a Required Aggregation Group and part of a Permissive Aggregation Group of plans and the Top-Heavy Ratio for the Permissive Aggregation Group exceeds 60%.

(c) Top-Heavy Ratio:

(1) If the Company maintains one or more defined contribution plans (including any Simplified Employee Pension Plan) and the Company has not maintained any defined benefit plan which during the five-year period ending on the Determination Date(s) has or has had accrued benefits, the Top-Heavy Ratio for this Plan alone or for the required or Permissive Aggregation Group as appropriate is a fraction, the numerator of which is the sum of the account balances of all Key Employees as of the Determination Date(s) (including any part of any account balance distributed in the five-year period ending on the Determination Date(s)), and the denominator of which is the sum of all account balances (including any part of any account balance distributed in the five-year period ending on the Determination Date(s)), both computed in accordance with Code §416 and the regulations thereunder. Both the numerator and denominator of the Top-Heavy Ratio are increased to reflect any contribution not actually made as of the Determination Date, but which is required to be taken into account on that date under Code §416 and the regulations thereunder.

(2) If the Company maintains one or more defined contribution plans (including any Simplified Employee Pension Plan) and the Company maintains or has maintained one or more defined benefit plans which during the five-year period ending on the Determination Date(s) has or has had any accrued benefits, the Top-Heavy Ratio for any required or Permissive Aggregation Group as appropriate is a fraction, the numerator of which is the sum of account balances under the aggregated defined contribution plan or plans for all Key Employees, determined in accordance with (i) above, and the present value of accrued benefits under the aggregated defined benefit plan or plans for all Key Employees as of the Determination Date(s), and the denominator of which is the sum of the account balances under the aggregated defined contribution plan or plans for all Participants, determined in accordance with (i) above, and the present value of accrued benefits under the defined benefit plan or plans for all Participants as of the Determination Date(s), all determined in accordance with Code §416 and the regulations thereunder. The accrued benefits under a defined benefit plan in both the numerator and denominator of the Top-Heavy Ratio are increased for any distribution of an accrued benefit made in the five-year period ending on the Determination Date.

(3) For purposes of (2)(i) and (ii) above, the value of account balances and the present value of accrued benefits will be determined as of the most recent Valuation Date that falls within or ends with the 12-month period ending on the Determination Date, except as provided in Code §416 and the regulations thereunder for the first and second plan years of a defined benefit plan. The account balances and accrued benefits of a Participant (I) who is not a Key Employee but who was a Key Employee in a prior year, or (II) who has not been credited with at least one Hour of Service with any employer maintaining the plan at any time during the five-year period ending on the Determination Date will be disregarded. The calculation of the Top-Heavy Ratio, and the extent to which distributions, rollovers, and transfers are taken into account will be made in accordance with Code §416 and the regulations thereunder. Deductible employee contributions will not be taken into account for purposes of computing the Top-Heavy Ratio. When aggregating plans, the value of account balances and accrued benefits will be calculated with reference to the Determination Dates that fall within the same calendar year.

The accrued benefit of a Participant other than a Key Employee shall be determined under (a) the method, if any, that uniformly applies for accrual purposes under all defined benefit plans maintained by the employer, or (b) if there is no such method, as if such benefit accrued not more rapidly than the slowest accrual rate permitted under the fractional rule of Code §411(b)(1)(C).

(d) Permissive Aggregation Group: The Required Aggregation Group of plans plus any other plan or plans of the Company which, when considered as a group with the Required Aggregation Group, would continue to satisfy the requirements of Code §§401(a)(4) and 410.

(e) Required Aggregation Group: (1) Each qualified plan of the Company in which at least one Key Employee participates or participated at any time during the determination period (regardless of whether the plan has terminated), and (2) any other qualified plan of the Company which enables a plan described in (1) to meet the requirements of Code §§401(a)(4) or 410.

(f) Determination Date: For any plan year subsequent to the first plan year, the last day of the preceding plan year. For the first plan year of the plan, the last day of that year.

(g) Valuation Date: The date elected by the Company in §2.35 as of which account balances or accrued benefits are valued for purposes of calculating the Top-Heavy Ratio.

(h) Present Value: Present Value shall be based only on the following rates: Interest rate: _____% Mortality table:________.

12.03. Minimum Allocation.

(a) The employer contributions and forfeitures allocated on behalf of any Participant who is not a Key Employee shall be less the lesser of 3% of such Participant's compensation or in the case where the Company has no defined benefit plan which designates this plan to satisfy Code §401, the largest percentage of employer contributions and forfeitures, as a percentage of Key Employee's compensation, as limited by Code §401(a)(17), allocated on behalf of any Key Employee for that year. The minimum allocation is determined without regard to any Social Security contribution. This minimum allocation shall be made even though, under other plan provisions, the Participant would not otherwise be entitled to receive an allocation, or would have received a lesser allocation for the year because of (i) the Participant's failure to complete 1,000 Hours of Service (or any equivalent provided in the Plan), or (ii) the Participant's failure to make mandatory employee contributions to the Plan, or (iii) compensation less than a stated amount.

(b) For purposes of computing the minimum allocation, compensation shall mean Taxable Compensation as defined in §2.30, limited by Code §401(a)(17).

(c) Neither Elective Deferrals nor Matching Contributions may be taken into account for the purpose of satisfying the minimum top-heavy contribution requirement.

Article XIII. Miscellaneous.

13.01. **Limitation of rights**. Neither the establishment of the Plan or the Trust, nor any amendment thereof, nor the creation of any fund or account, nor the payment of any benefits, will be construed as giving to any Participant or other person any legal or equitable right against the Company, Administrator or Trustees, except as provided herein, and in no event will the terms of employment or service of any Participant be modified or in any way be affected hereby. It is a condition of the Plan, and each Participant expressly agrees by his participation herein, that each Participant will look solely to the assets held in the Trust for the payment of any benefit to which he is entitled under the Plan.

13.02. **Nonalienability of benefits**. The benefits provided hereunder will not be subject to alienation, assignment, garnishment, attachment, execution or levy of any kind, and any attempt to cause such benefits to be so subjected will not be recognized, except to such extent as may be required by law. The provisions of the preceding sentence shall apply in general to the creation, assignment or recognition of a right to any benefit payable with respect to a Participant pursuant to a domestic relations order, except that if such order is a Qualified Domestic Relations Order, the provisions of the preceding sentence shall not apply.

13.03. **Failure to qualify initially**. If it is determined that the Plan or the Trust does not qualify initially under Code §§401 or 501, the Administrator will direct the Trustees to return to the Company all assets then held by the Trustees under the Plan within one year of such determination. Upon such payment, the Plan will be considered to be rescinded and to be of no force or effect. Any amounts returned to the Company under this §13.03 which are attributable to Elective Contributions or

After-Tax Contributions of a Participant shall be paid by the Company to such Participant.

13.04. Information between Administrator and Trustees. The Administrator and Trustees will furnish each other such information relating to the Plan and Trust as may be required under the Code and any regulations issued or forms adopted by the Treasury Department thereunder or under the provisions of ERISA and any regulations issued or forms adopted by the Labor Department thereunder.

13.05. Payment under Qualified Domestic Relations Orders. Notwithstanding any provisions of the Plan to the contrary, if there is entered any Qualified Domestic Relations Order that affects the payment of benefits hereunder, such benefits shall be paid in accordance with the applicable requirements of such Order.

13.06. Crediting of service with a predecessor employer. If the employer maintains the plan of a predecessor employer, service with that employer will be treated as service for the employer.

13.07. Control of trades or businesses by owner-employees.

(a) **Trades or business under common control.** If this plan provides contributions or benefits for one or more owner-employees who control both the business for which this plan is established and one or more other trades or businesses, this plan and the plan established for such other trades or businesses must, when viewed as a single plan, satisfy Code §401(a) and (d) for the employees of this and all trades or businesses. If this plan provides contribution or benefits for one or more owner-employees who control one or more other trades or businesses, the employees of the other trades or businesses must be included in a plan that satisfies Code §401(a) and (d) and that provides contributions and benefits no less favorable than those provided for owner-employees under this plan.

(b) **Trades or businesses that are not controlled.** If an individual is covered as an owner-employee under the plans of two or more trades or businesses that are not controlled and the individual controls a trade or business, then the contributions or benefits of the employees under the plan of the trade or business that are controlled must be as favorable as those provided for him or her under the most favorable plan of the trade or business that is not controlled.

(c) **Control defined.** For purposes of (a) and (b), above, an owner-employee, or two or more owner-employees, will be considered to control a trade or business if the owner-employee, or two or more owner-employees together: (1) own the entire interest in an unincorporated trade or business, or (2) in the case of a partnership, own more than 50% or either the capital interest or the profits interest in the partnership. For purposes of the preceding sentence, an owner-employee, or two or more owner-employees, will be treated as owning any interest in a partnership that is owned, directly or indirectly, by a partnership that such owner-employee, or such two or more owner-employees, are considered to control within the meaning of the preceding sentence.

13.08. Conflict with insurance contracts. In the event of any conflict between the terms of this plan and the terms of any insurance contract issued hereunder, the plan provisions will control.

13.09. Limit on rights conferred by this Plan. Neither the establishment of this Plan or Trust, nor any amendment thereof, nor the creation of any fund or account, nor the payment of any benefits, will be construed as giving to any Participant or other person any legal or equitable right against the employer, administrator or trustees, except as provided herein, and in no event will the terms of employment or service of any Participant be modified or in any way be affected hereby. It is a condition of this plan, and each Participant expressly agrees by his or her participation herein, that each Participant will look solely to the assets held in the trust for the payment of any benefit to which he or she is entitled under the plan.

13.10. Information sharing between plan administrator and trustees. The plan administrator and trustees will furnish each other such information relating to the plan and trust as may be required under the Internal Revenue Code and any regulations or forms adopted by the Treasury Department thereunder or under the provisions of ERISA and any regulations issued or forms adopted by the Labor Department thereunder.

13.11. Governing law. The plan and trust will be construed, administered and enforced according to the laws of [State] to the extent such laws are not inconsistent with and preempted by ERISA.

IN WITNESS WHEREOF, ABC Company, Inc. has caused this instrument to be signed by its duly authorized officer this ____ day of ______________, 19____.

ABC COMPANY, INC.
By: __________________

Appendix B
§401(k) Plan
Sample Employee Communications Material

Permissions and Disclaimer

This Appendix contains sample employee communications material used with a typical 401(k) plan. These communications materials are reprinted by permission of Tax Management Inc., a subsidiary of the Bureau of National Affairs Inc., Washington, DC. These materials are not intended to be accepted as the final word in either a legal or a technical sense. They are included for illustrative purposes only.

QUESTIONS AND ANSWERS ABOUT THE ABC CORP. SECTION 401(k) PROFIT-SHARING PLAN

I. General Facts About the Plan

Q-l: What is the Section 401(k) Plan?

A-l: It's a long-term way for employees of ABC Corp. to save for their retirement on a tax-favored basis. The Plan derives its name from the section of the Internal Revenue Code that authorizes such plans.

Q-2: Why did ABC Corp. set up the Section 401(k) Plan?

A-2: After Congress passed a law allowing companies to have such plans, ABC Corp. decided to implement the 401(k) plan because it is a benefit that allows you and other employees to save on taxes and, with ABC Corp.'s assistance, to save for retirement by investing in the Plan. Thousands of medium-to-large sized companies now have plans like this. What makes the ABC Corp. plan especially attractive is that, up to certain levels, if you elect to defer part of your salary into the Plan, ABC Corp. will match your contribution with a contribution of its own.

Q-3: I will have my Social Security benefit and my pension when I retire. Do I really need anything else?

A-3: Even with a good pension (ABC Corp. provides a pension plan for its employees and also makes contributions to the Section 401(k) Plan independent of any employee contributions) and Social Security benefits, you may still experience a reduction in your standard of living at retirement unless you have other resources. These resources can include personal savings as well as the equity in your home (for instance, if your home mortgage is paid off by the time you retire, you will need considerably less to live on). The Section 401(k) Plan is one means of helping you bridge the "gap" between your standard of living in the last several years of your employment (most likely, your most highly compensated years) and your standard of living once you retire. The Section 401(k) Plan benefit can also help you guard against inflation that may occur after you retire. What makes investing in the Section 401(k) Plan particularly advantageous when contrasted with other alternative investments are the following facts:

(1) Your Section 401(k) Plan benefit is indirectly subsidized by both the Federal and State Governments because, as further detailed below, employee contributions to the Plan will not be subject to income tax until they are withdrawn from the Plan. While these amounts are in the Plan, any interest earned on them will also not be taxed.

(2) Because the Section 401(k) Plan contains a matching feature, as further described below, ABC Corp. will help you save for retirement by matching, up to certain limits, any contributions you make to the Plan at the rate of $____ on the dollar. This gives investing in the Section 401(k) Plan a "leg up" on alternative investments.

Q-4: How does the 401(k) Plan Work?

A-4: Employees who are interested in investing in the Plan sign an agreement to have part of their salary contributed to an account in the Plan on their behalf. Instead of being subject to Federal and State income tax, as normal salary payments are, these contributions, unreduced by any income taxes, go into the Plan on your behalf. Thus, in a way, the Federal and State Governments pay a part of your retirement benefit for you by not taxing the amount you put into the Plan until years into the future. You will not have to pay income tax on these amounts until they are distributed to you (after you leave ABC Corp.). Further, for every dollar you put into the Plan up to ____% of your compensation per year, ABC Corp. will make a matching contribution to your Plan account equal to ____% of your contribution to the Plan.

Q-5: Are there any other special benefits to the Plan besides the fact that my contributions will not be taxed when made and the fact that ABC Corp. will add to my contributions by matching them as described above?

A-5: Yes. Because Federal and State income tax law encourages employees to save for their retirement, any investment return earned on your contributions and ABC Corp.'s contributions also will not be subject to Federal or State income tax while these amounts are held in the Plan. The advantage of this "tax-free compounding" of investment return over a period of years can be quite substantial.

In addition, if you have satisfied certain rules, any "lump-sum distribution" you receive from the Plan may also be eligible for special favorable Federal and State income tax treatment that can further reduce the amount of taxes you will pay when your benefit is distributed. The rules on eligibility for this type of favorable tax treatment are very complex, however, so you may wish to consult a tax adviser on this issue.

Q-6: Who can participate in the Plan?

A-6: All ABC Corp. employees who have completed one year of service and reached age 21 are eligible to make tax-favored employee contributions to the Plan and to receive ABC Corp. matching contributions. In addition, all employees who have satisfied the age and length-of-service requirements automatically will receive an ABC Corp. contribution on their behalf of ____% of their compensation per year, regardless of whether or not they make employee contributions to the Plan.

Q-7: When does my right to my Plan benefit become nonforfeitable?

A-7: Your own employee contributions will always be completely nonforfeitable. In addition, you will have a nonforfeitable right to any ABC Corp. regular contributions and matching contributions in your account after you have completed _____ years of service with ABC Corp.

Q-8: If I sign up for the Plan now, how long will this obligate me to make contributions?

A-8: Only until the next pay period. You may revoke your contribution authorization at any time and it will take effect in the following pay period. Employees who are not currently making contributions may sign up and have amounts contributed on their behalf as of the next pay period.

Q-9: How do I join the Plan?

A-9: Just fill out the contribution authorization form in the back of this booklet and deliver it to _______________. He will implement your authorization as soon as practicable, usually in the following pay period.

Q-10: Are there any limits on how much I can contribute to the Plan?

A-10: Yes. In any year, you cannot contribute more than 15% of your compensation from ABC Corp., nor may you contribute more than a stated dollar amount that is specified by law. For 19 __, that dollar amount is $____, and it is to be adjusted for inflation in later years. Also, if you qualify as a "highly compensated employee" under the Federal tax law due to your level of income and/or percentage of stock ownership in ABC Corp., the actual deferral that you are allowed to make may be less than the percentage and dollar limits described above because of the tax law's "non-discrimination" rules that apply to this type of plan. The deferral percentage allowed for certain highly compensated employees will depend on how much is contributed for the year by nonhighly compensated employees.

Q-11: Is there any minimum amount that I will have to contribute if I elect to make Plan contributions?

A-11: No. You may wish to start out slowly to see how your budget works, taking into consideration the Section 401(k) Plan contribution. The Plan permits you to do this and also permits you to vary the amount you put into the Plan as you go, so you are not "locked in" to any particular level of contributions.

Q-12: How will I know how much contributions and investment return I have in my Plan account at any point in time?

A-12: Once each quarter, you will receive a notice showing how much is held in your Plan account. If you want to know your account balance at any other time in the year, _______________, as Plan Administrator, will supply you with these numbers.

Q-13: If I have any further questions about the Plan, how can I get them answered?

A-13: Just fill out the Plan question form at the end of the booklet and give it to ___________________. He will get back to you with the answer.

Q-14: If I want to read more about the Plan, where can I get this type of information?

A-14: The Summary Plan Description (SPD) which has been mailed to you gives you additional details about the Plan. Also, ___________________ has a copy of the actual plan document on file in his office and will allow you to examine this document during normal business hours. Also, if you wish to have your own copy of the Plan, one will be provided you, but you may be charged a small photocopying fee.

II. Specific Tax Questions About the Plan

Q-1: I understand that I will not have to pay income tax on my salary deferrals until such amounts are distributed to me but, if I have to pay income tax on these amounts when they are distributed, how is that to my advantage?

A-1: First, the amounts held in your Plan account will grow free of income taxes. The effect of this "tax-free compounding" can be quite dramatic. It may even be possible to earn enough tax-free investment return on your money while it is in the Plan to pay any income tax due on your benefits when you receive them.

Further, if, at the time you receive a distribution, you are retiring, your Federal and State income tax on this money may be less than it would have been if you didn't sign up for the Plan and had to pay the tax now out of each paycheck, because you may be in a lower tax bracket when you retire.

Also, a special method for calculating your taxes can help you save taxes if you have contributed to the Plan for five years. This means any five years, not necessarily five years in a row. Called "forward averaging," this method can help you save taxes when you receive a "lump-sum distribution" from your Plan account (a payment of your total Plan benefit in a single year). In general, however, you may only use forward averaging once per lifetime and the employee for whose benefit the distribution is being made must be at least age 59½ and have satisfied certain other rules. It is important to get the advice of a tax professional to determine whether this method could apply to you.

Since the tax law is very complicated, it is impossible to state in a booklet of this nature what the exact tax consequences will be to any particular employee. Also, the tax law is constantly changing so by the time an employee receives a distribution, the law may be different. For the application of the Federal tax law to your particular situation, you should consult a tax adviser.

Q-2: If I receive a lump sum distribution from the Plan, do I have any other alternatives other than paying income tax on this amount in the year I receive it?

A-2: Yes. You may be eligible to "rollover" a lump-sum distribution to an IRA or to a new employer's qualified retirement plan (if such qualified plan accepts rollovers). If you do this within 60 days of receiving your distribution and the other tax law requirements for rollovers are met, then you will not have to pay income tax on the amount rolled over until it is distributed from the recipient plan. Note, however, that if you roll a lump sum benefit over into an IRA, this will generally mean that you will not be eligible for favorable forward averaging income tax treatment, as such treatment does not apply to distributions from an IRA. In addition, you may be able to achieve the same result by having the trustee of the Plan make a direct plan-to-plan transfer of your benefit into another qualified defined contribution plan, individual retirement arrangement, or annuity plan. Since it is impossible to describe all possible situations and their tax consequences, you should consult a tax adviser before deciding what you want to do with your plan distribution.

III. Effect of Making Plan Contributions on Other Benefits

Q-1: Will participating in the Plan in any way reduce the amount of Social Security benefits to which I will be entitled at retirement because my salary appears to be lower due to my Plan contributions?

A-1: No. Your Social Security benefit at retirement is based on your whole salary, including any amounts you defer into the Plan.

Q-2: Will I pay less Social Security tax if I sign up for the Plan?

A-2: No. Your Social Security tax, like your Social Security benefits (see Question #1, above) will be figured on your salary before anything is taken out for the Plan, so your Social Security tax (unlike your income tax) will be the same, regardless of whether you sign up.

Q-3: Will my election to make contributions to the Plan reduce in any way any ABC Corp. benefit to which I may be entitled?

A-3: No. Your ABC Corp. fringe benefits, such as health care and life insurance, are based on your total salary, including Plan contributions. Your decision to make Plan contributions will in no way reduce any of these benefits, nor will it in any way reduce the retirement benefits to which you will be entitled under ABC Corp.'s Pension Plan nor will it reduce the amount of Company contribution that you will be eligible to receive under the company contribution portion of this Plan.

Q-4: Will my election to make Plan contributions affect my ability to make IRA contributions?

A-4: In general, no, although employees who participate in an employer-sponsored retirement plan, such as this Plan, may not be able to fully deduct their IRA contributions for the year. This is because Federal tax law reduces the amount of deductible IRA contributions that an employee who participates in a qualified employer retirement plan may make, based on how much income those employees earn for the year. Since ABC Corp. employees are automatically enrolled in the employer contribution portion of this Plan as well as in the Pension Plan after completing a year of service and reaching age 21, these restrictions will apply to them anyway.

IV. How to Get Your Money Out of the Plan

Q-1: If I sign up to make contributions to the Plan, when can I get my money out?

A-1: You can get your money out only when you retire, or when you leave ABC Corp. in some other way, or in very unusual "hardship" situations.

Q-2: What is a "hardship" situation, and who decides?

A-2: The "hardship" standard in the ABC Corp. Section 401(k) Plan has to comply with IRS rules that cover all such plans. The plan administrator has the responsibility of determining whether a genuine "hardship," as that term is defined by the Federal tax law, exists whenever someone asks to take money out of their Plan account due to hardship. If the administrator determines that a hardship does exist, he will then determine what portion of the amount requested by the employee is required to meet the need created by the hardship, and will direct the plan's trustees to distribute this amount.

Q-3: What are some examples of a "hardship" that would qualify for a distribution?

A-3: A "hardship" generally must be something unexpected, such as a major loss not covered by insurance. Under Federal regulations, however, the following situations, if they give rise to a financial need, can constitute hardships:

1. education of a dependent of the employee;

2. purchase of a primary residence for the employee;

3. major medical expenses incurred by an employee or one of the employee's dependents which are not covered by insurance; or

4. any other cause which the administrator determines has produced an immediate and heavy financial need.

Q-4: If I were able to prove that I had a "hardship," could I take out all of my investment in the Plan, and would I have to pay a penalty?

A-4: You may only withdraw the amounts you yourself put into the Plan—not the ABC Corp. regular or matching contribution or any earnings on your Plan account.

Further, if you do receive a hardship distribution, you may have to pay the IRS a 10% penalty, in addition to having to pay income tax, on any amount received from the Plan (unless certain exceptions, such as for disability, apply, in which case the penalty may not apply, but regular income tax will still be due).

The hardship withdrawal rules make it more important than ever to think of the Section 401(k) Plan as a retirement fund, and to realize it will not be readily available to you while you work for ABC Corp. Therefore, it is important to put away only as much as you know that you can afford.

Q-5: If I were able to take my investment out because of a "hardship," and somehow I found I had enough money to take care of my problem some other way, could I put the money back into the Plan?

A-5: No, you could not put back any amount you had taken out for a hardship.

Q-6: Aside from hardship, what are the events that would entitle me to a distribution of my Plan account?

A-6: You may receive a distribution of your Plan benefits upon:

1. attaining "early retirement age";

2. attaining "normal retirement age";

3. becoming disabled;

4. ceasing to be employed by ABC Corp.

Q-7: What are "early" and "normal" retirement age under the Plan?

A-7: "Early retirement age," under the Plan is the later of the date you reach age 55 or complete 10 years of service.

"Normal retirement age" is the earlier of:

1. the date you reach age 65; or

2. if you begin participation in the Plan within five years of reaching age 65, the fifth anniversary of the date you began participation in the Plan.

Q-8: What qualifies as "disability" for purposes of the Plan?

A-8: The Plan defines "disability" as the inability to engage in any substantial employment-type activity, taking into account your age, education, and work experience, by reason of any medically determined physical or mental impairment that can be expected to last for at least 12 consecutive months.

Q-9: What are the forms of benefit distribution available under the Plan?

A-9: If you are married, the normal form of benefit distribution is a "qualified joint and survivor annuity." This is an annuity for your life or life expectancy coupled with, if you die leaving a surviving spouse, an annuity for your spouse's life or life expectancy equal to 50% of the amount that was payable during both spouses' lives. If you die while still working for ABC Corp., the presumptive mode of benefit payment is a "pre-retirement survivor annuity." A pre-retirement survivor annuity basically entitles your spouse to the benefit to which he or she would have been entitled if you had retired immediately before your date of death.

Employees also may choose among certain optional modes of benefit payments, provided they elect "out" of qualified joint and survivor or pre-retirement survivor annuity benefits in writing and such election is consented to by the employee's spouse (if any) in writing. Employees who have satisfied these requirements may choose to receive their benefits in any of the following forms:

1. A lump sum (except that this form is not available if you are receiving benefits on account of disability);

2. In substantially equal payments over a fixed period that may not exceed your life expectancy (or the joint life expectancies of you and your spouse);

3. In the form of a joint and survivor annuity, with the beneficiary being someone other than your spouse; or

4. In the form of a qualified joint and survivor annuity, except that the benefit payable during both spouses' lives will be reduced so that, if you die leaving a surviving spouse, your spouse, instead of the regular 50% benefit described above, will get either 75% or 100% of the amount payable during your joint lives, depending on which option you select.

Q-10: Can the Plan ever require me to take my benefit in a lump sum?

A-10: Yes, but only if the value of your benefit is $3,500 or less. If your benefit exceeds $3,500, then the Plan can only give you a lump sum distribution with your consent.

Q-11: What rights do I have to designate a beneficiary to receive any benefits remaining in my account upon my death?

A-11: If you are receiving joint and survivor or pre-retirement survivor benefits, this will happen automatically. If you are receiving benefits in some other form, and benefits remain due to you but unpaid at the time of your death, the Plan will pay any unpaid portion that is due to a beneficiary of your choosing. Once you choose a beneficiary, you can change beneficiaries by notifying the plan administrator in writing of the change.

Q-12: What happens if I die without leaving a surviving beneficiary and amounts still remain in my Plan account that are payable?

A-12: If you die and do not leave a surviving spouse or other designated beneficiary, then any remaining benefit payments due will be divided equally among your children. If such children are minors at this time, then a custodian or guardian may be appointed to manage the funds during this period. If you leave no surviving spouse, designated beneficiary or children, then, upon your death, any remaining benefits that are due under the Plan will be paid to your estate.

V. How to Sign Up

Q-l: How do I sign up for the Plan?

A-l: Use the authorization form at the end of this booklet. Fill in the amount you wish to invest in the Plan each pay period. Also, fill out the beneficiary designation form if this is the first time you have signed up for the Plan. If you have already filed a beneficiary designation form, you do not need to file another unless you wish to change your beneficiary designation. Give the completed forms to ______________.

Note that if you are considered a "highly compensated employee" for purposes of the Federal tax law, it is possible that the amount you contribute will have to be cut back to satisfy the nondiscrimination tests of Federal tax law. This cutback will be calculated by the plan administrator. Also, if you are a highly compensated employee and an excess amount is inadvertently placed in your account, the Plan will refund such excess amounts to you, together with any investment earnings on such amount while it was in the Plan. These amounts will be subject to Federal and State income tax.

Q-2: How do I change the amount I'm having taken out of my salary for plan contributions?

A-2: Just fill out another authorization form. Additional forms may be obtained from ______________________________. The form filed last in time will control.

Q-3: The beneficiary designation form says that I must sign it before a witness and get "consent" from my spouse (if you are married). What does that mean?

A-3: A plan representative must witness your signature. For this Plan, ____________ is a plan representative. By signing as witness, this person provides evidence that you signed the form yourself. If a plan representative is not available, you may use a notary public instead. If you are married and wish to name someone other than your spouse as your beneficiary, Federal law requires that your spouse must sign the consent at the bottom of the form and that the spouse's signature be witnessed by either a plan representative or a notary public.

Note: If you are naming someone other than your spouse as beneficiary, you will also have to elect out of joint and survivor annuity benefits—the presumptive mode of benefit distribution absent an election to the contrary. The beneficiary designation form allows you to do this, but any election not to receive benefits in joint and survivor annuity form must be consented to by your spouse if you are married, as described above. When electing not to receive benefits in the form of a qualified joint and survivor annuity, be sure to check the line beside the type of benefit payments you wish to select.

Q-4: May I change my beneficiary designation?

A-4: Yes. All you have to do is fill out another beneficiary designation form—the one filed last in time will control. Note, however, that if you are changing your beneficiary to someone other than your spouse, or electing to receive benefits other than in the form of a qualified joint and survivor annuity, your spouse must consent in writing to the change and this consent must be witnessed by a plan representative or a notary public.

Q-5: Where do I send the completed forms?

A-5: Send them to: ______________________

Answer Key to Questions for Review

CHAPTER 1

1. B
2. C
3. D
4. C
5. A

CHAPTER 2

1. C
2. D
3. C
4. D
5. A

CHAPTER 3

1. B
2. B
3. C
4. C
5. D

CHAPTER 4

1. C
2. D
3. A
4. D
5. B

CHAPTER 5

1. A
2. C
3. D
4. A
5. B

CHAPTER 6

1. B
2. D
3. D
4. A
5. C

CHAPTER 7

1. D
2. D
3. A
4. B
5. D

CHAPTER 8

1. A
2. B
3. D
4. B
5. C

CHAPTER 9

1. D
2. A
3. B
4. C
5. C

CHAPTER 10

1. A
2. B
3. D
4. C
5. A